The Author would like to thank the following people:

Stephen Fromstein and family

My family and friends

Susan and John Kersten

Facebook friends for the encouragement

The Creator for the amazing life I have had.

THE REAL ORIGIN OF MAN

One hundred and fifty years ago the theory I am about to tell would have seemed impossible. Today it is not only possible but probable. This story explains how we came into this earth as spirits as opposed to having evolved from apes. Interestingly, our current civilization is the only one ever to claim we come from apes. Virtually all other stories (usually called myths or legends) claim we were formed by a spirit race. In fact, the stories from the Sumerians, The Bible, and Edgar Cayce all say we were cloned by the Spirit Race. This book also delves into the idea that these spirits are still with us and shows how right up until World War 2 the "good" and "bad" spirits were still battling it out for supremacy. As I theorize, the events after the war show these "spirits" still want to control and run the earth. I will name the groups and individuals who are involved in this secret society.

The "myths" also all mention atomic bombs, space ships, airplanes and advanced technology that existed in our pre-history. Can all of these stories from different sources be wrong? And is it not possible that the technology we have today existed once before and we are basically re-living our past and trying to get it "right" this time? Also, all of these "myths" not only claim we came from the Orion galaxy or nearby galaxies, but all of these civilizations built pyramids; or even cities; that mimiced the layout of the Orion belt. Why would they do this?

I will talk about the Orion belt and all of these claims later as we discuss the various stories from the sources I use but when it comes to myths and legends, think about this. The first dinosaur bones were not discovered and recognized until 1841 and the first dinosaur bones in the USA were not discovered until 1858. Up until then, the idea that some animals weighed 20 to 80 tons was thought to be preposterous, if not an outright sign of insanity. Of course, today anyone denying the existence of dinosaurs would be thought to be crazy. That shows how history can change; and change dramatically; with one discovery.

As we develop scientifically, its interesting to note these so called myths become more realistic with each new discovery. As we delve into the story, we will also see how the Bible changed the story and coded certain aspects of the Sumerian Texts to hide the real story of Man. I hope those who believe the Bible will still read what I have to say and really think about what it says in The Bible. I am not prejudiced against anyone; believe in God; and am just presenting facts I have read and studied over the last 35 years. So first, lets have a look at how far and fast we have come in the last 150 years.

Lets say a family from the early 1800s was transported to current day America or most civilized countries. Look at what they would witness:

Cars, boats, trains, airplanes, computers, space ships, electricity, nuclear power, cloning, even the "God Particle" (Higgs Boson). They could watch TV and see a tape of man landing on the moon. Even though we looked like them, would they think we were some kind of gods? How could man come up with all these inventions in such a short time? Is it possible; as Edgar Cayce says; that many of us currently alive are reincarnations of spirits from Atlantis? And are the people; or spirits; of Atlantis the "gods" the Greeks and Romans speak of in their writings? There are thousands of unanswered questions about our beginnings and I will delve into some of them and see if we cannot come up with some answers. I suggest googling some of the information I present in order to advance your own knowledge about our mysterious beginnings as Man. It is a fascinating study as you will see.

Now imagine what we may invent in the next 150 years. Of course, we have to avoid destroying ourselves, which with modern technology is what could easily happen. So why would this scenario not be possible in our distant past? It not only is possible, it did happen and the various stories from the Sumerian texts, Edgar Cayce, the Hopi Indians and The Bible tells us exactly what did happen many centuries ago.

Let me quickly give a run through of who each of the above were.(I will go over the Hopi Indians in the discussion on their stories.)

THE SUMERIANS

According to historians, the Sumerians seemed to appear from nowhere about 3,500 BC. Nobody is quite sure where they came from or where they got the advanced knowledge they had. By 2,200 BC they had disappeared.

Considered the first civilization that left writings we can decipher and that have lasted, they wrote on clay tablets using reed styli. They wrote in a cuniform style using symbols instead of letters. For this reason, many of their writings can be deciphered in two or more ways. We will see how this impacted those who wrote The Bible. Make no mistake, The Bible is mainly taken from the Sumerian texts and later, from Gnostic Gospels. Once you see the similarity between Genesis in the Bible and the Sumerian texts, it will become apparent where the story of Adam and Eve and all the early Bible stories came from. I will also show how the Bible mentions aircraft, atomic bombs and other modern inventions that both the Sumerians and Edgar Cayce attribute to the Atlanteans or Anunnaki.

Much of the information on the Sumerian texts comes from a scholar named Zecharia Sitchin, who deciphered the Sumerian texts.

I believe the Sumerians actually were the direct descendants of the Egyptians, who in turn were taught; and lead; by the Atlanteans around 10,500 BC. I will go into much more detail when telling the story Edgar Cayce tells in the Chapter on "The Atlanteans and Egypt".

EDGAR CAYCE

Here is Cayces' exact quote from a reading concerning Mans' beginning.

Mans origin was as a spirit, not a physical body. These souls projected themselves into matter probably for their own diversion, interrupting an evolutionary pattern then going on in the Earth. Through the use of his creative powers for selfish purposes, man became entangled in matter or materiality to such an extent that he nearly forgot his divine origin of nature.

Cayce claimed he could read the Akashic Records. The Akashic Records were written on what Cayce called the "skein of time". The Hindus named the Akashic Records and were only one of many ancient religions who believed these records existed. These records are virtually every thought and act performed by every person on earth. Sound impossible? Well, Einsteins theory of relativity proved that atoms separated and even 3,000 miles apart, would still act exactly the same. In other words, if one half of the atom began circling counter clockwise suddenly, so would the other half atom 3,000 miles away. So, one part of our actions or thoughts remains on earth while the other is imprinted on "the skein of time".

Psalm 139:16 in the Bible gives a hint to the Akhasic Records. *"Every day of my life was recorded in Your book".*

Born in Hopkinsville Kentucky in 1877, Cayce had a few incidents in his youth that showed remarkable abilities. He could sleep on a book for instance and retain all the knowledge in that book. When in his young 20s, Cayce lost his voice for months and no cure could be found. A friend of his hypnotized him and incredibly, Cayce cured himself while in a hypnotic trance. He and his friend began trying this to cure other people and without fail, Cayce would find a cure for these people. Cayce cured over 2,000 people but one day a man named Arthur Lammers asked the hypnotized Cayce about reincarnation, Eastern religion and astrology. This began the over 5,000 "life" readings Cayce gave in his lifetime. The vast majority of these past lives occured during Atlantis and / or the time of Jesus. Here are a few of Cayces' predictions.

In the mid 1930s, Cayce predicted a shepard boy would find the Dead Sea Scrolls in 1947. He said they were written by the Essenes. At that time nobody had heard of the Essenes as they were written out of the Bible. They were an obscure Jewish sect that had split from the Philistines and the Sadducees. Their whole aim in life was to create an atmosphere for Jesus to enter into the world. Just as predicted, the Scrolls were found in 1947 by a shepard boy. They were written by the Essenes!

Cayce predicted in the early 1930s that lasers would be discoverd in 1959. Gordon Gould was given the patent for the laser in 1959 !!

Cayce predicted Atlantis would first reappear in 1968 or 1969 off the coast of Bimini. In 1969, land appeared off the coast of Bimini and many archeologists feel its part of Atlantis.

Cayce was a Sunday Bible teacher at his church and read the Bible cover to cover every year of his life from age 11. One can only imagine the horror he must have felt when his own readings while in a trance contradicted most of his waking beliefs and teachings. At first, not even Cayce could believe what he had said. However, the consistancy of the facts over the years convinced him he was right in his trance induced statements. We will see how his story of Mans beginning and the Sumerians and the Hopi are eerily similair.

THE BIBLE

The most interesting part of the Bible is this: The Bible claims Adam and Eve were the first man and woman but lets look at what happened with Cain and Abel. In Genesis 4:14 Cain says the following to the Lord:

"*All who see me will try to kill me*".

If Adam and Eve are the first humans and Cain and Abel are their first born sons, then who are these people who will try to kill Cain?

In Genesis 4:15, the Lord says, "*They will not kill you, for I will give 7 times your punishment to anyone who does*."

So right off the bat, we see the Bible has a credibility problem. There had to be other people on earth. Who were they? They were the Atlanteans (Anunnaki) !! Anytime you see the word Anunnaki it refers to the Atlantean race.

Oddly, the Bible leaves out all references to the spirit race, although they do mention angels often. I feel the Biblical angels are in fact the Spirit Race. The Bible also makes no reference to the Pyramids, the Sphinx or the fact Egypt had an advanced civilization during the time of the Bibles' Old Testament.

The reason is simple. The Bible was written around 70 AD, which is when the two factions (Jewish and what would become Christian) who had followed Jesus Christ, argued over whether one had to be Jewish to be "saved". When Jesus' brother James sided with those who became the Christians (who believed all could be saved regardless of race or religion), the Jewish sect split from them and wrote the Bible. They left out the spirit race,

Atlantis (The Bibles only reference to Atlantis is The Garden of Eden) and the advanced technology of the Egyptians and started The Bible with the creation of Adam. I suppose they felt it would not look good if the "choosen" people were way behind the Egyptians in technology and lifestyle. I do not want to judge whether the Jewish race are the choosen race or not, but Cayce said in a reading that The Lord would judge not on what religion you belonged to, but what you did on earth re your fellow man. So they may or may not be the choosen race, but these circumstances in 70 AD led to how The Bible was written.

More importantly, those who wrote the Bible did not want anyone to know the true story of mankinds beginnings. To this day, the Vatican has a secret library with books nobody is allowed to read. They admit the library exists but never say which books are in this library. Makes you wonder what these books say! Both the Sumerians and Cayce are adamant that the Spirit Race made Man and both tell similar stories to back up their claims.

Another thing to think about regarding the Catholic Church. Why did they never release the third secret given to the three young girls in Portugal at Fatima in 1917? The Virgin Mary appeared on the 13th of every month for 6 months. At least 70,000 people witnessed one or all of the visions. On the last visit, an incredible thing occured. The sun (after heavy rainfall) appeared to spin and land on the earth before taking its usual position a few minutes later. Witnessed by thousands, the Church wrote it off as aurora borealis, despite the fact Europe rarely sees this phenomena. By the way, the first secret was a vision of hell shown the young girls by the Virgin Mary. She showed them this pit of fire with souls burning in it and claimed this was the fate for those who were not devout.

The second secret claimed the first world war would soon end (it did in 1918) but if the Roman Catholic faith was not followed and Russia was not consecrated, a second world war would soon commence.

Despite a promise to release the third secret in 1960, The Vatican refused to release it and has never released the full text of the secret to this day. Again, one has to assume it has something to say regarding the Catholic Church that the Vatican does not want released. In 1981, the Vatican claimed the third secret was about the assassination attempt on Pope John Paul. They have never released the written account from Lucia (one of the 3 young girls who were given the secrets) to this day.

An interesting thing regarding this vision at Fatima. The young girls and all those who saw the vision (70,000 people in total) claim the Virgin Mary appeared luminous. The Buddist religion also claims there was a "luminous race". Cayce and the Sumerians also describe the Atlanteans (or Anunnaki) as luminous beings. The Bible claims Jesus appeared luminous to the Apostles upon his resurrection. This seems to verify that the Atlantean or Anunnaki were a spirit race.

The Bible also leaves out any mention of the Essenes, despite the fact Jesus was actually a member of the Essenes !!! As happens in any account of history, the "winners" tend to leave out the "losers". The Essenes had a difference of opinion regarding laws and beliefs of the other two factions, so split from the Philistines and the Sadducees. The main role of the Essenes (as they saw it) was to create an environment where Jesus could enter the world as Man and as the Son of God. To this day, other religions only consider Jesus to be a great prophet. Only the Christian religions believe Jesus is the Son of God.

Another interesting point regarding the Bible is that Jesus never once talked about forming a religion over what He preached. Jesus did not even follow the Essene religion. John the Baptist was known as the one who followed the Essene traditions and some claimed he was the Son of God and not Jesus. I believe the writers of the Bible purposely left out Jesus' affiliation with the Essenes as the writers belonged to the Sadducees and Philistines.

Even more interesting is the fact the Gnostics did not believe Jesus was Man but was a Spirit ! Needless to say, the Gnostics were completely deleted from the Bible in 325 AD when the First Council of Nicaea was held. This alone should raise questions among Catholics as to what did the Bible really say? How is it that a group of men; 325 years after the birth of Jesus; are able to change the Bible? Again, what are they trying to hide?

One thing these bishops and the Pope did in 325 AD was condemn Mary Madgelene as a prostitute. She was actually a businesswoman who gave a percentage of her profits to the ministry of Jesus. Even the Apostles realized Mary Madgelene was Jesus' closest associate. But for whatever reason, these bishops and Pope were intent on changing the role of women in the Church.

And then there is the story of Enoch. He is Noahs grandfather and tells an interesting story. Basically, he is taken "away from earth by God" in a "flaming chariot", never to return to earth. This book of Enoch "disappeared" and was rediscovered in 1821 by a professor at a Hebrew University. When the Dead Sea Scrolls were unearthed, they also contained the lost book of Enoch. Without a doubt, it describes what can only be called an abduction of some type. Was this the Atlanteans (Anunnaki) taking Enoch to Atlantis?

One last thing of note: The Bible talks about the "Fall of Man" and all of the ancient "myths" seem to say that Man was once incredibly advanced before falling into a period of darkness. Just one more thing that ties the Bible and these ancient "myths" together. Also, I saw the movie "Planet of the Apes" the other night and couldn't help but think of how the "forbidden zone" in that movie compares to how the Bible hides our past.

Anyways, as you can see, there are many many questions posed by the Bible and it is interesting to compare their stories to the Sumerian and Hopi Indian stories and also the psychic trances of Cayce.

I use the New Living Translation Bible for all of my Bible quotes in this book. I use Zecharia Sitchins translations of the Sumerian Texts. Lets start my theory or story off with the Sumerian Texts.

THE SUMERIANS / THE SPIRIT RACE

So far, historians have discovered about 500,000 cuniform writings from the Sumerians, but only about 25% of those have been deciphered. Most are bills of sale, tax reports, or accounting procedures of the day. This shows The Sumerians had an advanced, organized system of government and life, even back 5.500 years ago. But what is amazing are the texts which tell the story of how man began.

The Sumerian texts claim a group called the Anunnaki came from a planet named Nibiru. The word Anunnaki translates into English as "Those Who Came to Earth From Heaven". I believe the Anunnaki are the Atlanteans Cayce refers to in his readings. Whenever you see the word Anunnaki, think Atlanteans and the stories become very similar.

I believe the Anunnaki were what I refer to as the "Spirit Race". They still had a connection to the Creative Force and so were in that sense "gods" themselves. They had advanced knowledge of the universe and seemed to be like current Man in how they operated their society. The Anunnaki made Atlantis their headquarters. Over time, they used up the minerals in the Atlantis area so began looking elsewhere for what they needed. Incredibly, the Sumerians claim the Anunnaki lifestyle had burnt holes in the atmosphere and they needed gold to repair the ozone layer.

Even more incredible is the fact modern scientists feel shooting gold flakes into the air will reduce ozone layer depletion. Modern astronauts use a thin layer of gold on their helmets and visors and the spaceships are coated with a thin layer of gold to ward off ultra-violet light or radiation.

Although Sitchin mentions that the Anunnaki may have come to earth to rescue "lost souls", he dismisses the idea. I actually think this was one of the reasons the Anunnaki did come to earth. I will show why in the Edgar Cayce part of this story.

The Anunnaki decided on two areas of development. One was in Africa, which the Annunaki called *AB.ZU*. The other area was in the Middle East and was called *E.DIN*. Sound familiar? This area would be run by the Anunnaki leaders son Enlil and AB.ZU was to be run by his half son Enki. The leader of the gods or spirit race was named Anu. The Babylonians had a god called An so this "god" seems to have been around for quite some time in ancient history. I feel the "U" added to Anu denoted several gods. Among these gods were Enlil and Enki. These Atlantean gods were the gods of Greek and Roman "myths".

As we now get into the similarities between the Bible and the Sumerian texts, replace the word God with Enlil (the mean "God") or Enki (the kind "God") in Genesis and you see where the Bible gets its stories.

It turns out the Anunnaki workers hated the job of mining the minerals and Enlil was a complete tyrant as a boss. As a result, the Anunnaki basically went on strike and refused to do the work any longer.

Enlil was outraged and wanted to punish the workers but Enki was more understanding and came up with an idea. He had noticed some half human looking creatures (possibly homo habilis) and figured the Anunnaki could manipulate their DNA (as we can do today) and turn them into workers.

A meeting was called among the top Anunnaki leaders to discuss this idea but Enlil was dead set against it. However, Enki had his way and Anu decided they would develop these "creatures" into workers. Don't forget, Enki was running the settlement in Africa (*AB.ZU*) so the modern idea of man coming out of Africa is revelant. We just didn't come from apes, but were "cloned" by the Anunnaki. The Anunnaki decided to call these new creatures ADAMU. Note not only the name Adam, but just as Anu denoted more than one god, ADAMU means they developed "many Adams".

The Biblical writers translate the Hebrew word *avodah* (avod in Sumerian texts) to mean worship but it also means work. Its obvious; according to the Sumerian texts; that Man would be working for the Lord not worshiping Him. Here is the account written in Genesis 3:19

All your life you will sweat to produce food,until your dying day. Then you will return to the ground from which you came. For you were made from dust and to the dust you shall return."

The ADAMU did not really work out well, as they had short lifespans and were not intelligent enough to do the work properly or without getting injured or killed off. It was also taking up time and manpower to create the ADAMU.

Enki had another plan which involved allowing the ADAMU to procreate. Again, it involved DNA manipulation. A meeting was held once again among the Anunnaki leadership and Enkis' argument is detailed in Genesis 1:26:

Then the Lord (Enki) said, "Let us make people in our image, to be like ourselves." Note the Bible clearly states in OUR image not MY image, which is what it would say if there was one God involved.

Enlil was having none of it and argued in Genesis 3:22:

Then the Lord God (Enlil) said, "The people have become as we are, knowing everything both good and evil. What if they eat the fruit of the tree of life? Then they will live forever."

Enlil wins the arguement and ADAMU are cloned using Anunnaki sperm and a female ADAMU host. They call these new creatures ADAMA, which translates into English as "Man of Earth". Of course, with the Anunnaki living forever as spirits, even the ADAMA clones live to between 500 and 900 years until Noah. Check in Genesis 5:1 through 5:32 and it gives the ages of Adam and Eves' relatives.

According to the Sumerian texts, the Anunnaki word for the hospital where the cloning was done was SHI.IM.TI which translates into English as "the house where the wind of life is breathed in". Compare that to Genesis 2:7

"And the Lord God (Enlil) formed a man's body from the dust of the ground and breathed into it the breath of life." And the man became a living person." As the overall leader of the Anunnaki, Enlil would be in charge of the hospital so would be responsible for "breathing life" into the ADAMA.

Genesis 2:21 and 2:22 explains how woman (Eve) was made: *So the Lord God (Enki) caused Adam to fall into a deep sleep. He took one of Adams ribs and closed up the place from which he had taken it. Then the Lord God made a woman from the rib and brought her to Adam."*

The Sumerian word TI means both rib and life. So again, those who wrote the Bible took TI to mean rib while it actually means life. So if you read Genesis 2:21 and 2:22 it appears God (Enki) puts Adam under sedation (a deep sleep). He then took genetic material (life) from Adam, sewed him back up and presented Eve to him.

According to the Sumerian texts, the reason its Enki creating Eve is because he and a female medical doctor named Ninti are doing the cloning.

There are cuniform paintings dating from Sumeria that seem to show Enki and Ninti working by a table with medical looking equipment nearby. Could this be a painting of them at work cloning Man?

Some say Ninki (Enkis' wife) herself carried the ovum and she was known as the Moon Goddess. The Annunaki word for moon was Sin. So, as the Bible correctly states, Man was born in Sin !

One other Biblical clue that shows Man was first cloned, then allowed to pro-create occurs in Genesis 2:25, "*Now, although Adam and his wife were both naked, neither of them felt any shame*." They felt no shame because they did not have to have sex! They were still ADAMU. In Genesis 3:6 we see that Adam and Eve both eat from the apple from the tree of life and knowledge. As it says in Genesis 3:7 says, "*At that moment, their eyes were opened, and they suddenly felt shame at their nakedness.*"

The tree of life and knowledge is a reference to the Anunnaki DNA and once they "ate from the tree of life", they would be reproducing by having sexual intercourse. As Enlil states in Genesis 3:22, the ADAMA will "become as they are" if they eat from the tree. Enlil makes sure this isn't the case and oversees the cloning of the ADAMA.

Enlil decided to make sure these ADAMA knew their place and ordered that the birth of ADAMA would be long and painful. In Genesis 3:16 we see the following:

"Then he (Enlil) said to the woman, "You will bear children with intense pain and suffering."

It is obvious that before this, women did not have to bear children. That is because the Anunnaki could replicate. This might sound impossible until we look at Jesus and the loaves and fishes. How did Jesus take five fish and loaves and feed 5,000? He would have had to replicate both food items.

In order to teach the ADAMA how to do the work needed, the Anunnaki took them to their home (Atlantis) to learn the basics. This homeland was filled with gardens, lakes, trees, roads and all sorts of luxuries. Since the area the ADAMA would work was called E.DIN, this advanced, built up area was known as the Garden of Edin. (spelt Eden of course in the Bible). Once trained, the ADAMA were banished from the Garden of Eden (Atlantis) and sent to work in E.DIN.

The ADAMA continue to work for 1,650 years until the time of Noah and the flood. This timeline is actually laid out in the Bible in Genesis 5:1 through 5:32.

Here is the story of Noah from the Sumerian text.

Enlil hated sex and was upset to see the Anunnaki (Sons of God) having sex with the ADAMA (Sons of Man). It's ironic that even today, sex is somewhat of a taboo subject and causes many problems for couples or individuals.

In Genesis 6:3 we see the following: *"Then the Lord (Enlil) said, "My Spirit will not put up with humans for such a long time, for they are only mortal flesh. In the future, they will live no longer than 120 years*." Note Enlil refers to himself as a Spirit.

In Genesis 6:7 it says, *"And the Lord (Enlil) said, "I will completely wipe out this human race I have created. Yes, and I will destroy all the animals and birds too. I am sorry I ever made them. But Noah found favor with the Lord".* (Enki in this case, as we will see later).

In the Sumerian texts, Noah is called Utnapishtim. According to the texts, Enlil will cause a huge flood to occur. Again it sounds crazy until we realize two things: One, the USA used cloud seeding in the Viet Nam war to cause heavy rains.

Secondly, the US government has a program called HAARP that works on controlling the weather. Think of what effect controlling weather will have on war ! So again we see an idea that sounded preposterous just a few decades ago, is now possible and probable.

Getting back to the Anunnaki, Enki had "created" these ADAMA and felt not only compassion but felt they were part of him. As a result, Enki went to Utnapishtim and warned him about the flood and told him to build a boat. He gave Utnapishtim the exact dimensions. Enki also told Utnapishtim to bring the *seed* of each animal on board. While the Bible mentions the actual animals (7 of some, of which some are to eat, and two of each of the others) it makes no sense. How could a boat hold that many animals for any length of time? What would Noah feed the animals? How would Noah stop the animals from attacking each other if they escaped from their pens?

Also, Enki was the one who cloned Man, so he of all leaders would be able to assist Utnapishtim in this quest to bring the DNA (seed) onboard. I believe Utnapishtim (Noah) brought onboard DNA samples of all animals.

When Enlil saw that an ADAMA family had survived the flood he was furious. However, those with him talked him into allowing Noah and his family to live. After all, they would still need these ADAMA to work the fields.

Although Utnapisthim (Noah) was possibly among the few ADAMA left, there were still millions of Anunnaki left in the world. The survivors from the flood went to Eygpt and Central and South America. This accounts for the similiar type of pyramids found in both areas. Even many cities in the Middle East and Central America had similar names. For instance Chol was a city in Mesopotamia and in Central America there was a city named Chol-ula. Other similar sounding city names include Colua in Mesopotamia and Colua-can in Central America, Zuivana in the former and Zuivan in the latter. One other similar sounding city is Cholima and Colima. How is it that cities 8,000 miles apart, separated by an ocean, could have basically the same names? These names must have been important to the Anunnaki (Atlanteans), which is why they named cities after them.

There are many theories as to why prehistoric man built pyramids world wide and used the same dimensions when building them. Some were bigger than others but they all had the same shape and basic dimensions to size. Why? One theory is that the pyramids were some type of power source. Just as we cannot see television rays, there are obviously other invisible forms of energy. Naturally, television rays have been there forever, its just we had not "discovered" them or learned how to harness them, until the last 100 years or so. It would appear the Atlanteans figured out how to use some of these "invisible rays" to harness energy and power. By building these pyramids, did they somehow store energy in the pyramids? Were they like the nuclear reactors we have today?

Looking at Nikola Teslas inventions and theories of the late 19th century and early 20th century, it seems he may have been onto what the Atlanteans built around the world in prehistoric times. Tesla built a huge tower that could emit power to any object that came within a certain distance of it. It was known as the Wardenclyffe Tower Project and Tesla called this wireless transmission!! Unfortunately, Tesla was brushed aside due to the fame of Edison (whom he worked for at one time) and his own quirkiness. Ironically, his ideas seemed so far fetched, many thought he was insane. Today, we have caught up with Teslas ideas and have cell phones, IPads and all kinds of wireless gadgets. Despite making big money in the late 1800s and early 1900s, Tesla died broke living in a one bedroom apartment in New York in 1943.

Moving forward from "Noahs Flood" both the ADAMA and Anunnaki procreated quickly and cities began to spring up. Naturally, "Noahs Flood" did not leave just Noah and his family on earth. It did, however, destroy the three islands of Atlantis and the history of Atlantis as a continent. As we will see in the chapter on the Egyptians and Atlantis, the surviviors head to not only Egypt but to Central and South America and parts of the USA.

With the sudden explosion among the population, (as we have today) the Anunnaki decided to allow some of the ADAMA to become rulers over some areas. As usually happens, some of the ADAMA leaders got a little bit over ambitious and decided to build what the Anunnaki were building. And that was control towers and landing strips for the Anunnaki air ships! Don't forget, the Anunnaki were an advanced civilization much like we are today. Also, with the destruction of many cities, they would have had to re-build their infrastructure.

The Bible has one of the most perfect descriptions of an aircraft you will see in ancient texts. It is contained in Ezekiel 1:1 through 1:28.

In 1:19 it says, "*When they flew upward, the wheels went up too.*"

In 1:21 it says, "*When the living beings flew into the air, the wheels rose up*".

Verse 1:23 says, "*And under the firmament their wings were stretched out straight*". Verse 1:24 explains how they land, "*When they stood still, they let down their wings.*"

I don't know about you, but to me this is a perfect description of an aircraft.

Lets take a look at the story of the Tower of Babel. Babel means confusion in the Hebrew language.

Genesis 11:3 says: *"They began to talk about construction projects." "Come, lets make great piles of burnt brick and collect natural ashpault to use as mortar."*

Genesis 11:4 says: "*Lets build a great city with a tower that reaches to the skies*".

When you think about modern spacecraft leaving earth, they are brought into a tower that reaches towards the skies and then the rocketship takes off into the sky.

Genesis 11:6 says: "*Look" the Lord (Enlil) says, "If they can accomplish this when they have just begun to take advantage of their common language and political unity, just think of what they will do later. Nothing will be impossible for them."*

Rather than suddenly have Man speak many languages as the Bible states, Enlil scatters the various leaders to far flung areas so they can no longer communicate with each other. I take this to mean the ADAMA are starting to defy the Annunaki and trying to build their own cities and infrastructure.

These types of problems continued as Enlil and Enki and the other "gods" children began to grow up and be given areas to control or run. Jealousy, greed, anger and all the emotions we have today surfaced. Wars broke out between Enlils relatives and Enkis. Is it possible Cain and Able are used as the Biblical Enlil and Enki; or more likely; the Angels Gabriel and Lucifer? In the Greek myths, Enlil is Zeus and Enki is Poseidon.

According to Sumerian texts, Enlils' granddaugher Inanna marries a son of Enkis named Dumuzi. Despite the war between the two families, they allow the the marriage to proceed. Trouble ensues when Marduk (also known as Ra); Enkis first born son;

arrests Dumuzi and has him killed. Inannas family attacks Enkis family and all hell breaks loose.

The Bible actually covers many of these battles in Genesis 14:1 through 14:13. As the Bible seems to do, names are changed but these are the battles between Enlil and Enkis offspring.

Now comes the destruction of Sodom and Gomorrah. Abraham famously begs the Lord (Enlil) to spare the cities. The only reason Enlil will spare Abraham is that he had done work as an emissary and had commanded troops. Note Genesis 14:14 where Abraham (still known as Abram then) has 318 men he takes into battle.

Naturally, Enlil has no plan to save any people, he is bent on destruction.

In Exodus 19 we see how the men of Sodom want to have sex with other men and Lot offers up his two virgin daughters instead. This is the Bibles way of teaching how various sexual ideas are sins and that there is a steep price to pay for this kind of activity. The modern day Catholic Church (and many other churches) still claim homosexuality to be a sin.

In reality, likely both Sodom and Gomorrah were centres of commerce where Enkis' followers were building war materials. This made the two cities prime targets for attack. As with any big city, crime, poverty and prostitution were prevelant so the Bible uses this to explain the bombing of Sodom and Gomorrah. And make no mistake, the Bible gives an accurate description of an atomic bomb.

Genesis 19:24 says, "*Then the Lord (Enlil) rained down fire and burning sulphar from the heavens on Sodom and Gomorrah.*" He *utterly destroyed them, along with the other cities and villages of the plain, eliminating all life-- people, plants and animals alike." But Lots wife looked back as she was following along behind him, and she became a pillar of salt."*

Actually, salt back then was found in vapor pits so lets translate the last sentence of Genesis 19:24 with the proper wording. Just as the Bible writers misinterpreted other words in the Bible, they likewise translated the word for vapour as pillar of salt. Instead of being turned into a pillar of salt, Lots wife was vaporized.

Now, until Hiroshima and Nagasaki, we did not know people could be vaporized. Lo and behold, after dropping the two bombs on the Japanese cities, what did we see? People were literally vaporized and their shadows were imprinted into the ground.

And what did Abraham see the next day when he returned from the mountains where he had been told to hide out? According to Genesis 19:28, this is what he saw, "*He looked out across the plain to Sodom and Gomorrah and saw columns of smoke and fumes, as from a furnace, rising from the cities there."*

What else could cause not only two cities to be destroyed but all the surrounding landscape and life? And here is the final proof. Historians claim Sodom and Gomorrah were uninhabited for 240 years right after the time of the destruction. Also, scientists have lately discovered that the Dead Sea still has high levels of radioactivity! And one final proof comes from outer space. It seems airplane pilots and astronauts notice a weird thing in the Middle East while flying over. All the stones are blackened in the area of Sodom and Gomorrah! There is only one other area of earth where this occurs. The black rain that fell on Hiroshima and Nagasaki caused the stones in the area to blacken as well !!

The bombing of Sodom and Gomorrah seems to signal the end of Enlil and Enkis time on earth. Quite possibly, they lost complete touch with the Creative Force over such a hideous act as bombing two cities. Possibly, the story will continue once scholars have decoded more of the Sumerian texts. As we will also see in the Cayce story, it appears the Anunnaki (Atlanteans) lose their contact with the Creator and become Man. It definitely ends the first Pre-Sumerian civilization as the fall out from the bombs radiation blocks the sun and causes massive starvation and death. History shows at one point the number of humans on the earth had shrunk to about 1 million from a high point of 5 million. How did so many people disappear so quickly? An atomic or nuclear bomb and the subsequent fallout would certainly explain it.

One other interesting thing about the Sumerian texts. It seems the Sumerians not only knew about the planets Pluto, Neptune and Uranus, they knew their rotations and place in the sky. Considering you cannot see any of those three planets without the aid of a telescope, how did the Sumerians know about these planets? The information had to come from somewhere and most likely, it came from the Atlanteans. Where else could they get the information? Remember, the Sumerians were the first culture to write down any history, so its seems incredible they would suddenly know advanced scientific information like planet alignment.

Incredibly, the Sumerians also knew about the "long count calendar", which is the earths cycle over 25,920 years. The Mayans also knew about this calendar. How would two cultures so far apart know about a 25,920 cycle when in reality, neither of these cultures lasted anywhere near that long? One would assume the knowledge was passed down by a culture that DID last that long or longer.

One last note re the Sumerians. If they were so accurate regarding the calendars and the alignment of unseen planets, why would they not be accurate in telling the story of Mans beginning?

Now lets move on to the Hopi Indian story and its similarities to the Sumerian texts.

THE HOPI INDIANS

The Hopi lived in what is now Utah, New Mexico, Arizona and California. They descended from a group called the Anasazi. The Hopi Indians claim a civilization known as the Ant People saved them from the first destruction of the world by helping them hide underground or in caves. The Hopi claim the this destruction was caused by fire and volcanoes.

The Hopi word for ant is ANU ! And the Hopi word for friend is NAKI !   So the story the Hopi tell and the one the Sumerians (and Cayce as we will see) tell are virtually the same. To me, that is undeniable evidence that this destruction did occur in our pre-history. And what does the Bible say?

Numbers 13:33 says the following, *"We even saw giants (Nephilim) there, the descendants of Anak."*   (Anunnaki ??)

Did the Bible writers use the word "Anak" to mean the Anunnaki? The word Nephilim in Hebrew means "those who have fallen".   Some Bibles use the word Nephilim and others use giants. If we use the proper Hebrew translation for Numbers 13:33 it would mean "we even saw those who had fallen (to earth), the descendants of Anak." Here is another reference to the Anunnaki from the Bible. Deuteronomy 2:10

The Emims dwelt therein in times past, a people great, and many, and tall, as the Anakims." Some Bibles use the word Anakites as opposed to Anakims.

I realize its not proof but Anakims and Anunnaki are close and they refer to them once again as tall and that there were many of them.   The more you study the Bible, the more it seems to point to an ancient race that was tall and had a large population and "fell" to earth.

I believe the Bible really does mimic the Sumerian and Hopi story, it just uses slightly different names and descriptions of events. Possibly the writers of the Bible did not know what to call the advanced inventions of the Atlanteans or covered up the information to make it appear "God" had created or done these things. This is NOT to say there is no God. The Atlanteans (Anunnaki) were simply spirits from God who formed on the earth. This is basically what the Bible and Cayce say as well.

So it would seem both the Bible, Cayce, the Sumerians and the Hopi Indians refer to a race that had "fallen to earth" and intercoursed (in more than one way !!) with those on earth. Since the Hopi come from a tribe known as Anasazi, it seems to be telling the same story. As we will see, Edgar Cayce claims the Atlanteans escaped the first destruction on earth by fleeing to the Americas and hiding in caves!

I know many will doubt any civilization was living in the USA that far back but a United Press story in 1954 claims a doctor by the name of J. W. West found pieces of human leg bones in Louisana that dated to 50,000 BC. In 2004, Dr. Albert Goodyear did radiation tests on carbonized plants and them to be 50,000 years old, which he says means Man was in the Americas in 50,000 BC minimum. It seems every few years, Mans beginnings are found to be further and further back in time than we knew.

The Hopi legends mention how the ant people arrived on these "big birds". It seems when they left, a "small bird" was on top of the "big bird" and after take off, the small "bird" would fly away as the "big bird" became tired. Does this not sound like modern day spaceships? We piggy back a smaller rocket onto the back of a bigger one and after take off, the smaller craft lifts off into space, leaving the big one to eventually fall to earth. Remember, the Hopi at this time had never seen or built these kind of things, so would write something other Hopi could relate to (in this case a bird) to try and explain what they were seeing. Interestingly, a Welsh legend from ancient times tells the exact same story and the Iroquois Indians also have a similar tale.

According to Hopi legend, the second civilization of Hopis were much advanced over the past generation. They built cities, buildings and traded with other nations. Obviously, this was because the Atlanteans (Annunaki) were helping them. However, as they became more wealthy, greed began to seep into their culture. Wars broke out and then a weird thing happened. It seems, according to the Hopi, that the world went crazy and began rotating wildly. Volcanoes, tsunamis, earthquakes rocked the earth and an ice age occured. Again, this sounds exactly like what happens when the North and South Poles switch places. Cayce makes the exact same claim in his readings. Cayce puts this period at about 28,000 BC.

Scientists also know the switching of the poles has happened before and it will happen again.

The third destruction was caused by a huge flood according to Hopi legend. Not only that, they describe the third generation of Hopi as an advanced civilization with rapidly growing cities and populations, increased trading and a "patuwvota", (which meant "shield of hide") which could fly through the air and was used in warfare.

According to Hopi legend, the people became so corrupt, selfish, wicked and warlike that their world was ended by a huge flood.

In Hopi legend, they tell of how Sotuknang (Hopi God) twice destroyed the earth through fire, then ice. Sotuknang saved the few good people both times by hiding them underground with the ants!! When they came out after the flood they saw the huge islands (Atlantis?) had sunk.

As you can see, these "myths and legends" start to show a similar pattern over and over.

So there you have the Hopi legend showing 3 distinct destructions over a 40,000 year period.

Here are a couple of other interesting stories put forth by the Hopi. One story says Man must never bring back anything from the Moon or else "the balance of natural and universal laws and forces would be disturbed resulting in earthquakes, severe changes in weather patterns, and social unrest".

I don't think I would be surprising anyone by saying our weather is getting whackier by the year. As for social unrest, it is interesting how our society has changed so dramatically since the late 60s. From jobs galore, benefits and an unseemingly brilliant future, look at the world today.

Back in the 60s we had the hippies who promoted peace and love. The hippies had long hair, wore colorful clothes, had no jobs and lived in communes. Could the hippies be a reincarnation of the followers of Jesus? And the American government a reincarnation of Roman rulers?

Realistically, the only two cultures to ever have men with short hair are the Roman Civilization and our current civilization from 1919 onwards. Before 1919, look at pictures of US presidents or world leaders. Longer hair, sideburns, moustaches, beards were all common. Go right back through time and men always had long hair (except the Romans). Then, once World War One ended, short hair became the norm for men.

Compare that to the Romans. Short haired men (they were continually at war as America seems to be today) with the same white toga as a uniform or standard style of clothes. Along comes Jesus and the Apostles and they have long hair, beards, moustaches, wild colored robes or togas. And just like the hippies, they had no jobs and no place to live (they stayed at followers communal homes or slept in the desert according to the Bible).

But even worse to the Romans, they were promoting peace !! Just as America makes it money from war, so did the Romans. Just as the hippies got in the way of running a war, so did Jesus and the Apostles get in the way of Roman wars. And just as the American (and Europeon and British) governments waged war on the hippies and peace protesters, the Romans persecuted Jesus and his followers. Its odd when you think about it. Why would governments attack, arrest and even kill innocent people who want to end wars? As a modern day example, look at John Lennon. Not only did he have the same appearance as Jesus with his beard and long hair, he also actively promoted peace. And what happened to Lennon? He was harassed and followed by the FBI and CIA, denied entry to the USA and when finally allowed into the USA, was killed by a "follower". It would appear some things never change ! Jesus was turned in by one of his biggest followers, Judas.

We have also seen a tremendous shift in wealth and power over the last 40 years. The middle class is eroding, the wealth is mostly shared by the top 1% of the population and workers are continually given less job security and benefits. Granted, nobody can say all this happened just because we went to the moon and brought back rocks, but the Hopi Indian prophecies seem to be eerily accurate.

The Hopi also claimed that if plants began to bloom in the middle of winter, suffering and destruction were on the way. The last few years, we have seen plants begin to blossom way earlier than ever before.

The Hopi also believed they were from the Constellation of Pleiades. Note what it says in Job 9:9 in the Bible: *He made all the stars, the Arcturus, the Orion, the Pleiades and the constellations of the southern sky."* (Some Bibles use Bear instead of Arcturus, however, Arcturus is known as the Bear.)

Amos 5:8 says, *"It is the Lord who created the stars, the Pleiades and the Orion."* You do have to wonder why the Bible only mentions these constellations among the utterly millions of constellations we know exist in the universe today.

Here is an Edgar Cayce quote regarding Man coming from Arcturus:

As indicated, or as has been indicated in other sources besides this as respecting this very problem, - Arcturus is that which may be called the center of this universe, through which individuals pass and at which period there comes the choice of the individual as to whether it is to return to complete there - that is, in this planetary system, our sun, the earth sun and its planetary system - or to pass on to others. This was an unusual step, and yet a usual one.

The Sumerians claimed the Anunnaki came from Nirubu. Was this also a reference to the Orion Belt?

One way or the other, all ancient stories claim we come from "somewhere else" and the Hopi, Cayce, and the Bible all make it clear that someplace else is the Pleiades / Orion Belt / Arcturus.

We also see many examples of old structures from ancient times that mimic the Orion belt. The pyramids for one, whole cities in Mexico and Egypt, Stonehenge and even stones found near Lebanon (most likely erected during the Phoencian dynasty) mimic the Orion Belt.   As you see, these structures literally cover the whole world, not just one region or area.

I suppose the main question is, why did ancient man make so many structures that looked like and were arranged in the same structure as the Orion Belt? You have to think there is some kind of connection, otherwise, why go to all the trouble of making various structures so closely resembling a far off star galaxy?

Another amazing thing about all of these old important "ancient sites" is that they all line up within one tenth of one degree of each other. If you drew a line through the earth, it would line up the following: The Sumerian city of Ur, the Easter Island statues, Stonehenge, Machu Picchu, Nazca Lines, the lost city of Petra and the temples of Angkor Wat among others.

Now lets look at the story Edgar Cayce told in his "readings" or trance induced state. The similarities to the Sumerian and   Hopi stories are astounding.

EDGAR CAYCE

In his readings, Cayce claimed Spirits created Man, man had developed nuclear power and bombs and that 3 destructions over 40,000 years rocked the earth. These predictions match the Hopi Indian stories exactly. Many of Cayces readings also match the Sumerian history as told in their texts. So is it just coincidence or is there something to these "myths and legends"??

A timeline for Mans entry into earth would be as follows according to Cayce.

Around 10 million years ago, spirits had entered the earth and began entering into; then becoming stuck; in animal bodies. (materiality). They tried to metamorphisize into the human form but could not (being separated from the Creator) so created the various half animal / half man beasts we see in cave paintings or exist in Greek or Roman "myth" legends or stories. Among these would be satyrs, centaurs, gargoyles, mermaids and other "deformities" created by these spirits entering into animal forms. There would also be giants and midgets. Here is a Cayce quote from a reading:

"In Atlantean land in those periods before Adam was in the earth, among those who were then thought projections and the physical being had the union of sex in the one body, and yet a real musician on the pipes or reed instruments."

Note how Cayce mentions at this point that these "projections" do not have to have sex, but procreate as amoeba do. Also, you can't help but be reminded of the story of Pan in the Greek myths when reading the above reading given by Cayce. And remember, the Anunnaki did not have to have sex to procreate until creating

ADAMA, only animals had to have sex to procreate.

Another Cayce life reading says this: *"In the Atlantean land during those periods when there were the encasements and indulgencies of many that had put on matter or material bodies.*

Getting back to Mans timeline, as these spirits stayed longer and longer in the animal bodies, they became stuck in materiality.

Another group of spirits; lead by an Atlantean named Amilius; saw what was happening on earth and decided to try and rescue these "lost souls".

The first thing these spirits, or spirit race, had to do was come up with a human form that was consistant. Here is Cayces quote from a reading given to an individual in the mid 1930s:

"*in the days when the Sons of God came together to reason in the elements as to the appearance of man in the physical on earth's plane and this entity was among those choosen as the messenger to all the realm."*

Here is another reading from Cayce regarding forming man:

"*In Atlantean land when there were the separation of bodies as male and female"*.

So just as the Anunnaki formed Man (ADAMA) through the cloning of their own DNA and that of a "lesser creature", Cayce seems to be claiming the same thing.

Moving forward, some of the Spirits who came to rescue man (known as the Sons of God in the Bible) became caught up in earthly pleasures such as sex and food and began losing their connection to the Creator. These spirits created a world similar to ours and did so very quickly, much as we have done in the last 150 years.

This created a division among the Spirit Race. Having created Man or the human form, some of the Sons of God wanted to use these "Sons of Man" to do work while they took it easy and partook of the pleasures of life. This included sex with human females as the Bible states in Genesis and as the Sumerians say in their story of the Annunaki. Note the Sumerians also claim the Annunaki used these "lesser beings" to do work for them. Other Sons of God remained true to their original plan, which was to save Man and have them re-connect with the Creator. Cayce says these two divisions were called "The Law of One" (those who believed in the Creator) and the Sons of Belial, who did not believe in the Creator anymore. Here is a Cayce reading showing that:

"In Atlantean land before Adam ---timekeeper for those who were called things or servants or workers of the people---entity felt need of change or reform so that every individual would have the right of choice or freedom---felt desire to improve the conditions for the worker---felt need of God's hand in what evil or Satan had brought in the earth."

Interestingly, the Dead Sea Scrolls refer to two groups known as the Sons of Darkness and the Sons of Light. Speaking of the Dead Sea Scrolls, they were discovered over 65 years ago yet where are the translations we were promised? There are only minimal translations from the Dead Sea Scrolls. Why are they being covered up and what might the Dead Sea Scrolls say about our ancient past? Again, you have to wonder who is it that does not want this information out in the public?

According to Cayce, the Law of One won out and decided to choose one form for humans and created all five races at once and they refered to them as Adam.

Here is the quote from the Cayce readings showing where Man would be located on earth:

"As we find, those in the Gobi, the yellow; the white in the Carpathians; the red in the Atlantean and American; the brown in the Andean; the black in the plain and the Sudan in African."

Were Enki and Enlil the leaders of the "Law of One" and "Sons of Belial?"   Cayce only mentions the names of the individuals who are requesting a reading so he never mentions Enki or Enlil or any leaders of Atlantis. He does give the Atlantean names to hundreds of those asking for life readings. Here are a few examples of Atlantean names: Asmen-n , Deui, Lus-Lu, Atlan, Hept-supht, Ai-Ellaiin and Miium. Cayce also mentions a ruler from India named Said. In another reading Cayce says the following:

"In the period then---some hundred, some ninety-eight thousand years before the entry of Ram into India."

Among the countries Cayce mentions during these ancient times include Og, Mu, Poseidia, Lemuria, Om, Oz, Aryan and of course Atlantis. Twice in readings, Cayce mentions a city named Eden in Poseidia.

Just before we get into the three destructions described by Cayce, I want to show what Cayce had to say about our death and what happens when Man passes on.

Basically, Cayce claims when we pass on, we stay within our

solar system until we have "learned the lessons we need to learn" and then we pass into the Arcturus / Orion galaxies and have no need to return as a human being or form.

Cayce says these are what the planets in our solar system represent:

Pluto: subconcious

Jupiter: strength

Mars: anger

Neptune: mysticism

Mercury: mind

Venus: love

Uranus: psyche

Saturn: woes

Earth: testing

We would need to go to the planet that would teach us what we need to learn from our last life. So if you were lousy at love, you would spend time in the atmosphere or sphere of Venus to learn about love. If you wanted to learn more about mysticism, you would spend more time around Neptune. To sharpen your mind for your next incarnation, you would head to Mercury. Sure this may sound dumb or silly, but why do almost all religions claim we leave our bodies at death and go to the "spirit world"?

The Biblical heaven is actually Arcturus and purgatory is our own galaxy.

Both Cayce and Hopi Indians claim the seven endocrine glands tie us to the Creator. Cayce also claims The Book of Revelation in the Bible shows the connection between the seven endocrine glands (called the seven seals in the Bible) and the Creator. When you read Revelation you will notice everything is in sevens. Seven angels, seven plagues, seven gold lamposts, sevenfold Spirit, seven churches, seven stars in his right hand. The Eastern Religions call these chakras. They are as follows:

The seven endocrine glands are the pituitary gland, the pineal gland, the thyroid gland, the thymus, the adrenal glands, the lyden gland, and finally the sexual glands (the testes or ovaries).

Now lets look at the three destructions as given in the hundreds of readings describing the life of the Atlantean civilization. Just like the Hopi, Cayce claims the three destructions occured over a 40,000 year period from roughly 50,500 BC to 10,500 BC.

The first destruction occurs when Cayce says huge animals threatened to overrun the earth. Cayce gives an exact date of 50,722 BC. Cayce says the world leaders at the time had a meeting.

Cayce describes an airship called the Graf that picked up other world leaders and brought them to the meeting. The Germans named their airship the Zeppelin Graf !! Here is the Cayce reading describing how the Atlantean leaders were going to handle this problem.

"*And this was administered much in the way or manner as if there were sent out from various central plants that which is termed in the present the Death Ray, or the super cosmic ray, that will be found in the next 25 years.*"

The laser was invented in 1959, 25 years after this reading!

However, before this plan could be implemented, Mother Nature interrupted (or possibly the lasers that were used caused unforseen destruction) and destroyed much of the earth at the time. It also drove many of the people of Atlantis and other counties (Mu, Og, Lemuria etc as previously mentioned) to the Americas.

Here is a quote from the Science Daily:

May 18, 2010 — An international team of scientists has discovered that climate change played a major role in causing mass extinction of mammals in the late quaternary era, 50,000 years ago. Their study, published in Evolution, takes a new approach to this hotly debated topic by using global data modelling to build continental 'climate footprints'.

Once again we see science catching up with Cayces' life readings and facts.

Here is another reading from 1944 from Edgar Cayce:

"In Indian land when Said was ruler----among those who gathered to rid the earth of enormous animals which overran the earth but ice, nature, God changed the poles and the animals were destroyed, though man attempted it at the time."

It would appear Cayce is claiming the poles switched, causing massive tsunamis, volcanoes and earthquakes.

Cayce claims Atlantis was now broken up into five islands. Notice how he mentions inventions we have discovered today. This reading was given in 1941.

"In Atlantean land just preceding the first break up of the land when there was the use of many of those influences that are again being discovered that the Sons of Belial turned into destructive forces-------could be benefits to communcations and transportation etc. "

In other words, this is likely lasers or nuclear power Cayce is refering to and just as occured in 50,722 BC, we are facing the same decisions today. Nuclear power and lasers can be of great help to mankind or it can destroy mankind.

Note how this ties in exactly to the Hopi legend. The group called the ant people (Annunaki or Atlanteans) comes over and saves the Hopi by telling them to hide in caves or underground. I would assume this means some kind of radiation or possibly volcanic dust has covered the earth so they have to stay out of the wide open spaces.

The Atlanteans slowly recover over time and build their civilization back up to what they had around 50,000 BC. During this time the Law of One and Sons of Belial continue to disagree and argue and war breaks out here and there, much as we see on todays earth.

Here is a reading from 1938 that describes what was happening in Atlantis just before the second destruction: *"And there were those, with the entity and its associates or companions, who left the activities to engage in the building up of the activities in the Peruvian land. For the Atlanteans were becoming decadent, or being broken up owing to the disputes between the children of the Law of One and the children of Belial." (470-22 July 5, 1938*)

Another reading tells of impending doom:

"In Atlantean land during the periods of exodus due to the foretelling or forordination of activities which were bringing about destructive forces. Among those who were not only in Yucatan but in the Pyrenees and Egyptian land, for the manners of transportation and communications through airships of that period were such as Ezekiel described at a much later date."

So Cayce verifies that Ezekiel was talking about airplanes or airships !

Cayce claims this second upheaval occured around 28,000 BC. Here are quotes from readings regarding that time period:

"In Atlantean land at time of second upheaval, counselled those making exodus to other lands."

"In Atlantean land when peoples understood the law of universal forces ---entity able to carry messages through space to the other lands, guided crafts of that period."

Just as the Hopi Indians talked about the earth spinning out of control and becoming ice, Cayce also claims an ice age destroyed parts of Atlantis. Interestingly, scientists claim the Neanderthals disappeared around this time. Were the Neanderthal the "things" or "automatons" Cayce talked about and were they the ADAMU the Sumerians claimed the Anunnaki cloned? Its an interesting thought. After the Neanderthals disappeared we see the rise of the Cro-Magnons, who were much more 'human like". The Cro Magnons may have been the ADAMA.

This second destruction reduced the Atlantis area down to three islands. These islands were Poseidia, Aryan and Og.

Despite all this destruction, the Atlanteans still had an advanced civilization according to many Cayce readings. Here is a reading from 1935.

"In Poseidia the entity dwelt among those that had charge of the storage of the motivative forces from the great crystals that so condensed the lights, the forms of the activities, as to guide the ships in the sea and in the air and in conveniences of the body as television and recording voice."

A crystal is an organized grouping of atoms or molecules. Therefore we use crystals in many products today. However, Cayce is specific in that these "great crystals" would help ships and airplanes and be used in television and recording techniques. Cayce may have been refering quartz crystals when he said "great" crystals. Today, quartz crystals allow us to make all kinds of super powerful watches, computers, ships, guidance systems etc.

Television itself was not really popular until the 1950s and this reading was given in 1935. The current LCD televisions did not really become popular or well known until recently. The LCD stands for Liquid *Crystal* Display. It also sounds like he is describing a GPS system re guiding ships and airplanes. And remember, we are talking about Atlantis around 30,000 BC here !!

With this second destruction of Atantis, once again many inhabitants escaped to the Americas and to Egypt and the Middle East. They maintained an advanced civilization as we see from the buildings left behind in Mexico, Peru and other areas of Central and South America. Incredibly, many of these advanced buildings still stand today. They are the same pyramid shape as those in Egypt and many other areas of the world. Many of those buildings also are arranged in the exact order of the stars of Orion ! You really have to wonder how they built buildings that can stand over thousands of years when modern day man has trouble building anything that lasts more than 200 years !! Look around North America and see how many buildings from 1813 are left standing.

Also, we do not build any buildings today in the pyramid shape. Many scientists now theorize that the pyramids were some sort of power plants. It would explain why they were built worldwide and in the same shapes.

The Hopi; as noted previoulsy; also claimed after this second destruction that the society that emerged was advanced. Nations traded, air and sea travel was extensive. The only drawback seemed to be this third civilization still had problems between the Law of One and the Sons of Belial.

The greatest example of proof for an advanced ancient civilization between 28,000 BC and 10.500 BC is Puma Punku, in modern day Bolivia. Proven to be built around 17,000 BC, these 800 Ton blocks of stone are carved to precise right angles. All scientists who have studied these stones say the same thing: They had to be cut with lasers and diamond cutters. Scientists who cut stone with modern day lasers and diamond cutters compared the details with the bricks from Puma Punku and they show the *exact* same cut and look. And what could these massive stone blocks be used for?

According to the show "Ancient Aliens", (which I love but I do have one complaint which I will share below) it turns out the Germans had secretly built landing and take off pads during World War Two for their V1 and V2 rockets and they looked exactly like the stones and layout at Puma Punku. I notice the show Ancient Aliens never mentions Atlantis, only aliens from other galaxies. There were no aliens showing Man all of these things or teaching them this information. All of this technology and information came from the Atlanteans here on earth. When you watch Ancient Aliens (and again, its a great show) just replace the word "Alien" with "Atlantean" and you will see how much of this book matches up with what the show says about mans past history.

Sure, most of the ancient "myths" and stories tell of how we came from the Pleiades as spirits but according to Cayce, no other planet or galaxy anywhere has human type life. Spirits form according to the atmosphere and conditions of each planet or moon or sphere.

Now we move to the third and final destruction of Atlantis. This occured about 10,600 BC to 10,500 BC and is recorded in the Bible as Noahs flood.

Before we delve into that, let me point out Cayce claims Adam and Eve were put onto earth around 12,000 BC. According to Cayce, an Atlantean spirit named Amilius saw that the Annunaki were becoming more like humans or ADAMA and losing their connection to the Creative Force. (God, Buddha, Mohammad, or whichever name one wishes to call the Creator). This meant the Atlanteans (Anunnaki) were now; more and more; having sex to procreate instead of replicating. They were losing their spirit "form" and becoming Man.

As a result, this Atlantean; Amilius; offered to enter into sin or selfishness and become Man. Cayce does not say if this is done through reincarnation or possibly using the sperm of Amilius to impregnate an ADAMA female or simply having his DNA cloned. As I will discuss in the chapter on Jesus, Cayce claims Adam was one of the incarnations of Jesus Christ.

Again, I realize all this may sound like some sci fi movie, but in reality we can clone humans today, although governments have outlawed it for the most part. In reality, Adam may have been the first cloned person! And is this why the Catholic Church has a secret library of banned books and is so dead set against science? If Adam and Eve were cloned (and I believe they were) that changes everything we have been taught in modern society.

The timing of all of this certainly fits according to the Bibles timeline. It appears to be 1,656 years between the "birth" of Adam and Noahs Ark. Plato claims Atlantis was sunk about 10,500 BC, just as Cayce does. If Adam appeared about 12,000 BC, then subtract the 1,656 years and you come up with 10,500 BC basically.

This flood was caused by the melting of the ice from the ice age that started around 12.500 BC. With farming becoming popular, that heated up the earths surface and ended the ice age before it really took hold. The resulting melting sank the remaining islands of Atlantis. We would be wise to think about how global warming is melting the glaciers in Antarctica and the Arctic and what the results might be.

The Atlanteans fled to Egypt, South and Central America and what are now parts of the USA.

One quick note before we move onto the Atlanteans in Egypt. Scientists have wondered what it is that causes the Bermuda Triangle to cause havoc with compasses and even make ships or airplanes disappear. Going back to Cayces readings about the advanced civilization of Atlantis, is it possible the Atlanteans had invented some sort of power source or energy or even power plant that still exists beneath the waters?   Is this what causes all the weird goings on over the Bermuda Triangle? Many claim the Pyramids are power generators or plants. Its an interesting thought and I wonder if any scientists have delved into this possiblity?

THE ATLANTEANS AND EGYPT

With the final destruction of Atlantis, the remaining survivors flee to Egypt and the Americas. There is also an influx into Egypt of peoples from India, Mongolia and other regions affected by this massive flood.

By this time (10,500 BC) the Atlantean people had lost the ability to replicate and were now Man as we are today. However, they still retained extensive knowledge and brought this knowledge with them to Egypt.

Now, lets take a quick look at the history of what was happening in the region just before and during the Great Flood.

A group from the Carpathians; lead by a priest named Ra Ta; invaded Egypt. Ironically, in a reading given for himself, Cayce claimed to be Ra Ta in a past life !! Ra later became a "god" to the Egyptians and his son was Horus, who became Osiris. Osiris married his half-sister Isis according to Egyptian lore. If you google Ra you get many discrepencies over exactly who or what Ra was, but Cayce is consistent in his story of Ra and his place in Egyptian history tied into being the main negotiator between the Atlanteans and Egyptians.

Here is something that really makes one think: Some scholars claim the name Israel is taken from the following three people: Isis, the queen mother of Egypt; or *issa* (which means woman in Hebrew); from Ra, the above mentioned god, and from EL, which is the Hebrew name for God. So we have IS RA EL......the mother, father and God. Certainly an interesting thought.

There were already tensions and outbreaks of civil war and violence between the ruling class and natives of Egypt. Add to this the influx of a new race and the potential for disaster was high.

Before the influx of Atlanteans arrived, the ruling class had managed to have Ra Ta banished from Egypt and sent to Abyssinia. Ra Ta was promoting the idea of one God, while the Egyptians worshipped the sun and various gods. According to Cayce, the Egyptian population still had some of these "things or automotons" among its peoples. They had various appendages (scales, feathers, tails) on their bodies from their days of entering materiality.

It was obvious to the native Egyptians that the Atlanteans were much more advanced scientifically than they were. The Atlanteans also brought over their "things or automotons" to do the work for them. The Atlanteans looked down on the Egyptians and tried to set up a society or area separate from the Egyptians.

Already having a civil war amongst themselves, the rulers of Egypt quickly saw the Atlanteans could overpower them easily. The Atlanteans considered the Egyptians no better than the "things" they had brought over.

The former enemies within Egypt decided to band together and approach the Atlanteans for help in advancing their society. Once they saw the Atlanteans had a belief in one Creator, it was decided to bring back Ra Ta as a mediator.

This was successful and a decision was made that the three factions would work together and form a better society for all of them.

Here are a number of Cayce readings to give an idea of what was occuring during this time:

"in the Atlantean land before the third destruction---------assisted Alta, the scribe, in preparing a history of the land."

With the realization of the children of the Law of One that there was to be the final breaking up of the Poseidian-Atlantean lands, there were the emigrations with many of the leaders to the various lands".

"Conducted people from Atlantis to Egypt previous to last destruction----worked with adorning buildings with gems or precious stones".

"Came into Egypt from Atlantis when very young in years, became what today would be an instructor in psychological tests."

"An Atlantean who came to Egypt, aided in styling for dress and conveniences for home".

"In Egypt, one of the guards sent with the priest to what is now Abyssinian land during nine years of priests banishment."

Cayce claims the Atlanteans built two hospitals to cure the Egyptians once and for all from their hinderences or animal like appendages. One hospital was called the Temple Beautiful which is where they operated on the Egyptians and removed tails, scales, tumors or whatever leftover appendages they had from entering into materiality all those centuries before.

I know this might sound ridiculous but remember the cave paintings. There are literally thousands of cave paintings depicting Egyptians (and others)with scales, wolfs heads, feathers, hoves and various animal like appendages. Why would they paint these thousands of pictures if they were not reality?

The other hospital was called the Temple of Sacrifice. This was more of a psychological hospital where the Egyptians were taught sociology (how to raise a family as they did not live in one family group at the time but nomadic groups), spirituality (worship of one God) and an overall upgrading of basic knowledge, especially mathematics.

Here is a quote from a reading: *"In Egyptian land during periods of rebuilding of material, religious and social order, reared with children of young king".*

The Cayce reading below sounds quite a bit like the Annunaki and what they did:

"entity part Egyptian and part Atlantean----associated with activities when there was the preparing and presenting of ways and manners in which the race might be changed".

I should note that many of these readings are given five, ten or fifteen years apart yet the information, names and places are always 100% consistant. Either Cayce was reading the Akashic Wall or he had the best memory on earth.

With the peaceful agreement between the three factions, Egypt now entered an incredible phase of development. They developed a common language based partly on the existing Egyptian language and partly on the Atlantean language. This language was passed down to the Sumerians, then the

Phonecians and became the basis for our language today. Hence the word phonics !

With the increase in intelligence of the local Egyptians and the Atlantean knowledge, a decision was made to build the Sphinx and the Great Pyramids. These were built between 10,490 to 10,390. Granted modern day scientists say the Pyramids were built around 2,500 BC to 4.500 BC but I believe Cayce will be proven correct. Graham Hancock; a noted author on our pre-historic past; claims the pyramids replicated the night sky over Egypt in 10,500 BC. !! Many other scholars feel the pyramids were built on wet ground. Was this wetness from the Great Flood? Egypt is basically a desert today, so this may be another clue to the Pyramids and Sphinxs real date of creation.

Regarding the time frame for building the Pyramids and Sphinx, the Sumerians are known to have existed from 3,500 BC until overrun by the Semites, Akkadians and the Babyalonians around 2,200 BC and neither of these cultures mention building any pyramids !! Scholars say the Egyptians built the Pyramids and Sphinx, but fail to say where they learned the techniques that would allow them to build such advanced structures.

For instance, the Pyramids use Pi and supposedly Pi was not "discovered" until the Greek mathematicians around 2,000 BC. (and all of the Greek mathematicians went to Egypt to obtain their knowledge). The Pyramids also give the *exact* dimension of the earth, its longitude and latitude and its 365 day cycle around the sun. Now how would the Egyptians in 2,500 BC know about Pi or all of the other intricate information that can be obtained from the Pyramids? This incredibly advanced information had to come from an advanced civilization. Also, believe it or not, the

Pyramids were the only structure on earth that could be seen from the moon in 1969.

To me, the answer is obvious. The Pyramids and Sphinx were built by the Atlantean population who fled to Egypt after the Great Flood. Look at the figure known as the Sphinx. It is half man (the head) and half beast (a lion). The Egyptians still had the vestigages of those animal appendages when the Atlanteans arrived. So was the Sphinx built to show the coming together of the Egyptians (the lion) and the Atlanteans (some feel the head is a depiction of Ra)? Cayce claims the people of Atlantis wrote a detailed account of Mans existence from the beginning as spirits and it is buried near the right paw of the Sphinx. Cayce says it will be discovered by the reincarnates of those who originally put it there or had a hand in writing the records.

As to how they were built, Cayce was quite specific. He claims the Pyramids were designed and built (as the overall supervisor) by a man named Hermes with the help of Ra Ta. The Greeks have a god named Hermes so I wonder if it is the same man?

As to how they moved the giant stones Cayce is once again specific. Here is the quote from a Cayce reading:

"By the use of those forces in nature as make for iron to swim. Stone floats in the air in the same manner. This will be discovered in '58."

In 1958, a German physicist named Werner Heisenberg, developed what is called the Unified Field Theory. Heisenberg was the leader of the German atomic committee during World War Two. The Unified Field Theory is tied to quantum mechanics but so far nobody has figured out how to apply it to make huge stone structures float. According to Cayce though, this is how the "Egyptians" (actually Atlanteans) built the

Pyramids and Sphinx. So if there are any scientists reading this book, Cayce has given some clues as to how we will discover how to make stones float through the air !!

Here is a quote from Your Dictionary Biography regarding Heisenberg introducing the idea in 1958, just as Cayce predicted!

After World War II Heisenberg did much to reorganize scientific research as head of the Max Planck Institute of Physics and of the Alexander von Humboldt Foundation. In the early 1950s Heisenberg turned with great vigor toward the formulation of a "unified theory of fundamental particles," stressing the role of symmetry principles. This theory was intensively discussed at an international conference in 1958, the year he moved to the University of Munich as professor of physics.

Looking back for a second, just as the Sumerian texts and Bible talk about nuclear weapons and war and destruction, Cayce does as well. Lets look at some quotes given by Cayce:

'In Atlantis before the first of the destructive forces; entity builded those that made for the carrying these machines of destruction that sailed both through the air or under the water.' (1735-2; 10/16/30)

man brought in destructive forces to be used by people that were rulers. These destructive forces combined with those natural resources of the gases, of the electrical forces made in nature, caused volcanic eruptions...we find in various portions of the world, even in the present day, some form of legend of these events referring to an 'Eden' of the world.' (363-4)

there was the creating of the high influence of radial activity from rays of the sun that were turned on crystals...' (263-4; 3/6/35)

.electrical forces that dealt with transportation of craft from place to place, photographing at a distance, reading inscriptions through walls even at a distance, overcoming gravity itself,

preparation of the crystal, the terrible mighty crystal; much of this brought destruction.' (519-1; 2/20/34)

Cayce does not give a year for this nuclear destruction but mentions "Eden", which would put the destruction close to the Sumerian (and Biblical) timeline. Cayce also gives a pretty good description of how bombs were made and transported. Dont forget, these readings were given in the mid early to mid 1930s (dates are shown on 3 of the above readings) which was before the atomic bomb was developed. Also, Cayce mentions that the Atlanteans had lasers as far back as 50,722 BC !

Cayce also mentions "overcoming gravity" which I take to mean the Atlanteans had discovered anti-gravity.

Unfortunately, the building of the Great Pyramids and Sphinx marks the beginning of the end of the great Atlantean / Egyptian civilization. History has no record of any invasions or internal bickering among the people of Egypt but I think we can be pretty sure there was plenty of both, as we see from studying the history of any civilization. Whatever happened, the knowledge possessed by the Atlanteans seems to have slowly disappeared over 1,000 years. By 9,000 BC, the Egyptians are no longer building structures like the Pyramids but seem to be simple farmers and craftsmen.

The biggest change in Egypt was the change from the belief in one God to the belief in many gods and the sun. The Pharaohs were considered "gods" and lived forever according to Egyptian lore.

Looking at some of the Egyptian "gods" we see some interesting names. For instance, the mother of gods was called Anat. Not far off from Anak, the Nefilim (Annunaki) mentioned in the Bible. The King of Gods on Earth was called Horus, who was also considered the son of Ra. Re was the Sun God. These names were conjured up thousands of years after the building of the Pyramids and Sphinx, so its interesting how it seems certain names were passed down through the ages.

What is the most fascinating thing of all is this: The Greek mathematicians all went to Egypt to learn about math and then came back to Greece with this knowledge. So obviously, some Egyptians had retained advanced mathematical knowledge.

The best known Greek philospher, mathematician and all round genius was Plato. In Egypt he studied geometry, astronomy, geology and religion under a man named Sechnuphis. This is no doubt where he heard the "legend" of Atlantis. Plato also brought back advanced ideas on how to structure a society. Law, courts, philosphy and government were just a few of the areas Plato touched on. The Atlanteans of course taught the Egyptians these ideas centuries before Plato arrived.

Archimedis (born 287 BC) went to Alexandria were he was educated as a young man. He "discovered" the Archimedis Screw, but is has since been discovered this knowledge was known in the 7th Century BC. This shows the knowledge the Greeks obtained from Egypt went way back in time. He also invented the basics of levers and used huge mirrors to reflect sunlight onto oncoming Roman ships to destroy them. These ideas were all in place in Egypt in 10,500 BC and used to build the Pyramids. The knowledge was kept alive all those centuries by a few people (Masons as we will see) and passed onto people like Archimedis. Another Greek who studied in Alexandria was Hipparcus, who was an astronomer, mathematician and geographer.

Also, the Greeks designed some of the most advanced buildings of their time. This was something else they learned from the Egyptians. The Acropolis, The Theatre of Dionysia and the original Olympic Stadium were all based on Egyptian knowledge. As with almost all of the other ancient buildings built using Egyptian knowledge, some remains of these buildings still stand today.

So, it is obvious the knowledge the Atlanteans passed on to the Egyptians was still alive ten centuries later in Greece. Now lets look at Roman society.

In 45 BC, Julius Ceasar hires an Egpytian named Sosigenes to develop a calendar. This becomes known as the Julian calender but is produced from knowledge the Egyptians had and the Romans obviously did not have.

The Romans also went to Egypt to learn how to build big stadiums such as the Coliseum. Holding 55.000, parts of this stadium still stands today. The Pantheon, the Roman Forum, all of these buildings used Egyptian technology and parts of these buildings are still standing today. The Baths of Caracalla are still used today and it was built in 216 AD !! You just have to marvel at how all, or parts, of these buildings can still be standing today. And you have to believe whatever technology the Egyptians were passing on to the Greeks and Romans was advanced. Realistically, more advanced than todays buildings. So how did the Egyptians obtain the knowledge? It had to be passed down through the ages but it would appear only a small group had retained this knowledge. They were called masons and formed guilds.

History shows us the first masons or guilds in Rome date back to 715 BC under a ruler named Noma Pompilius. The masons still exist today and are still a secretive society.

Is it possible these masons or guilds were also passing on knowledge of the "spirit world" that shaped or created human life? I will show shortly how World War Two was actually a battle between the "Atlantean bloodlines" but first lets look at the Man who was sent by God to rescue Man.

JESUS CHRIST - THE PERFECT SPIRIT

The first thing we learn about Jesus is that he was not conceived. This puts him in the same realm as the Spirit Race, who were not conceived but entered materiality. Cayce notes that Mary, His mother, was also an Immaculate Conception. I wonder what their DNA would have been? Also; another clue to His being a spirit; Jesus appears as a spirit to the Apostles after his death. This (along with His birth) is called transfiguration.

Check this quote out from Edgar Cayce when discussing Anne (Marys' mother) and Immaculate Conception:

"...that Anne proclaimed the child (Mary) was without father. It's like many proclaiming today that the Master was immaculately conceived. They say, "Impossible. It is not in compliance with Natural Law." It is a Natural Law, as has been indicated by the projection of mind into matter."

So Cayce reaffirms that spirits entered into materiality. Jesus did exactly the same thing. He entered directly as a fetus (as opposed to being conceived) and was born a man.

It had been 10,000 years since Noahs flood and mankind was becoming more and more "lost' and losing touch with The Creator. This is why Jesus was sent to earth. He was to show the way back to the Spirit World from where Man first started.

Cayce also claims Jesus had 29 other incarnations before becoming the Perfect Man or Jesus. One person asked Cayce during a reading if he would attain perfection in this lifetime. Here is the reply from Cayce:

"Why should you expect to do in one lifetime what it took the Master 30 lives to attain."

Among those incarnations were Amilius, Adam, Melchizdek, Joseph, Joshua (son of Nun, who was associated with Moses), Enoch, Zen (father of Zoroastra), Job, David, Hermes (who built the pyramids), Asaph and Jonah. Lets take a look at the similarities between Jonah and Jesus' lives.

Both fell asleep on the ship during a raging storm. Both awaken to quell the storm. Both are headed to (and land) in Spain. Although the Bible says Jesus was on the Sea of Galilee, the surrounding landscape makes it impossible to be Galilee. Modern archeologists place Spain as the place Jesus landed after quelling the storm. Most interesting, Jonah spends three days in the whales stomach, much like Jesus spent three days before his resurrection. If you look at the Hebrew translation of the story of Jonah, it turns out this "whale" has shiny bronze skin. It sounds much more like a submarine than a whale. The fact the "whale" deposits Jonah on the beach also sounds like a submarine coming to shore and dropping Johah off. So was Jonah one of the incarnations of Jesus?

I wonder who else was an incarnate of Jesus. One candidate would be Akhenaten. The Egyptians had gone from the worship of one God to worshipping the sun and numerous gods. Suddenly, after centuries, Akhenaten reverts back to believing in one God. He names the God Aten.

Akhenaten was originally called Amenhotep 1V but changed his name to Akhenaten. One translation of Akhenaten into English (among others) is "Son of God". After his reign, Akhenaten was stricken from the Egyptian records and they went back to their multiple god beliefs.

Some historians claim Akhenaten was actually Moses. Both were saved by being floated down the river in a reed basket. Moses is identified in the Bible as a high ranking Egyptian. Moses helps some shephard girls chase away other shepards and feed their sheep and they tell their father Reuel this. Here is Exodus 2:19:

"*An Egyptian rescued us from the shepards", they told him.*

In Exodus 2:20 the father (Reuel) says: *"Go and invite him home for a meal".* Moses ends up staying at the house and eventually marries Reuels' daughter Zipporah.

So does the Bible once again hide or obscure facts? It would not look good if an Egyptian Pharaoh was the leader of the Jews or was involved in communicating with God and receiving the 10 Commandaments.

Moses was also taught in the "Mystery Schools" (in the Pyramids) mentioned by Cayce. If one studies the Egyptian Book of the Deads ten rules for living and the Ten Commandaments, its obvious how similar they are. So were the 10 Commandaments just a re-writing of the Egyptian Book of the Deads 10 rules for living? An interesting thought and evidence seems to point to this being a fact. As a matter of fact, the 10 Commandaments were not written in the Hebrew language but in Egyptian hieroglyphs. The Hebrew language did not come into existence for another 1.000 years after Moses received the Commanadements. In reality, the 10 Commandaments were likely a list of laws or ideals to be followed by the Israelites. The "landing" of God on the mountain seems to compare to the landing of a rocket ship. Moses enters the ship, disappears for 40 days and comes back with the Commandaments. Were the 10 Commandaments simply a set of rules handed down by the Atlanteans to the Israelites? It all seems very mysterious and becomes more complicated when you realize Moses kills a man. How is it a murderer becomes one of the most saintly persons in Biblical history? Exodus 2:12 shows how Moses killed the man. *"And he (Moses) looked this way and that way and when he saw that there was no man, he slew the Egyptian and hid him in the sand."*

Speaking of the Egyptian Book of the Dead, Raii would be another candidate as an incarnate of Jesus. He wrote the Book of the Dead.

One more interesting person who could have been a re-incarnation of Jesus is Mohammed. Alive around 600 BC, Mohammad was a great prophet and had encounters with the angel Gabriel. As a matter of fact, the Islamic and Catholic (Biblical) religions have much in common. Its too bad the various religions worldwide continue to argue over whose God is the "real" God.

Another interesting point on the life of Jesus concerns the missing years between ages 12 and 30 that the Bible leaves out. Why did the writers of the Bible leave out this critical information? Cayce goes into detail about these missing 18 years.

It turns out Jesus spent those 18 years being educated. Ironically, He studied astrology, numerology and astronomy, all subjects the Catholic Church frowns upon. I have to assume that is why the Bible "left out" these important years in the development of Jesus. Among his teachers were

JUDY: She spent 5 years teaching Jesus astrology and prophecy.

KAHJIAN (in India) studied the cleansing of the body as related to physical and mental strength.

JUNNER: studied in Persia under Junner. Was taught the teachings of Zu. When I googled Zu, I found he was the servant to Enlil !!!! His full name was ANZU, which translates to "know heaven". Apparently, according to legend, Zu stole the "Tablets of Destiny" from Enlil. Were these what Jesus was taught? The main thing is this continues to show the existence of Atlantis or the Annunaki. Remember AN from the Babylonian religion and ANU from the Sumerians? All similar names and actually; for whatever reason; virtually all of the gods or races from pre-history seem to start with the letter A. Annunaki, Atlanteans, Adam, Anu, Anasazi, Anzu, Adama, Akhenaten, Angels, the list goes on.

EGYPTIAN TEACHINGS: Jesus was in the same classes as John the Baptist according to Cayce. They were taught many of their classes inside the Pyramid. The teachings in the Pyramid were known as the "Mystery Schools". This shows that Jesus was being taught the advanced technology and mathematics of the Great Pyramids and also shows the intensive teaching Jesus received over the 18 years he traveled and was educated. Moses and Plato are among others educated at the Mystery Schools. Basically, these schools taught about immortality, numerology, advanced mathematics and architecture, astrology, astronomy, geometry, Mans place on earth and what happens when Man passes on. They purportedly also were taught how to cure disease, raise the dead, control the weather, levitate and psychic ability. If you look at the history of Jesus, he could do all of those things. Jesus studied Eastern Mysticism and a religion called Jainism as well.

According to Cayce, Jesus represents all religions that follow the adage God is One. Remember, Jesus did not start any religion. He studied most of the religions of the day and then began his own ministry at age 30. His ministry was based on those tenets he spent 18 years learning.

Remember at His birth, the three wise men showed up to pay homage? How did they know where Jesus was to be born? Cayce says it was psychic ability and names two of the three wise men. Here are some quotes:

"*and through the application of those forces----as ye would term today psychic---we find them coming to the place where the child was.*"

"Achlar was the wise man who brought incense to the child Jesus. For he lived in a period which has meant and does bring hope to the world."

Cayce claims Achlar was from Persia and was a sage who taught the mathematical methods passed down from Zend, Og and Uhjltd. He also taught astrological and natural laws.

"*Ashtucil was from India and brought the frankincense to Jesus.*

The third wise man came from Egypt. As a footnote, when in

his trance state, this kind of information came out quickly and even if asked 15 years apart, Cayces' answers were exactly the same. Names, places, dates, everything was always the same.

Cayce also claims Jesus had 2 brothers and a sister. His brothers were James (who became the head of the church after siding with those who became Christians), Jude (who became one of the 70 later "apostles" sent to preach the word of Jesus) and Ruth. Ruth did not meet Jesus until Joseph (their father) died. Jesus was 19 at the time and returned from his studies in Egypt. Ruth had heard both good and bad things about her brother and according to Cayce, was in awe at meeting Him. Those saying bad things were the Jewish leaders who later condemned Jesus for claiming to be the "King of the Jews". The Jewish leaders had a deal with the Romans: They could keep their beliefs, holidays and synagogues as long as they did not have a king. The Romans knew any race could get behind a king and revolt so had made deals with all of the countries they conquered: No king and you can keep all of your beliefs. If you declare a king, you will be attacked and destroyed. It appears the Jewish leaders helped the Romans corral Jesus and keep the Romans up to date on His whereabouts and His teachings.

Another interesting theory among scholars is the idea of the Merovingian bloodline. What happened to the descendants of Joseph, Mary, Ruth, Jude and James? If Mary was an Immaculate Conception, her DNA might be different than all others and who today possesses that DNA?

Many scholars say the family of Jesus escaped to France and continued their bloodline there. These descendants were called Merovingians and were considered descendants of King Meroveus.   They were known for their esoteric knowledge and occult practicies.   Members of the Priory of Scion claim to have knowledge of who is related to Jesus and his family to this day. If you saw the movie; or read the book; The DaVinci Code, you know about this idea. They claim Mary Magdalene and Jesus were husband and wife and had a child. They claim Mary Madgelene was pregnant when Jesus was crucified. She escaped to France after the death of Jesus and mixed with the Franks to form a bloodline that ruled France for centuries. I do not believe this myself but I am trying to put across as many ideas as I can in this book to allow the reader to delve into whatever facts they want to follow up on.

PRIORY OF SION AND THE PROTOCOLS

The Priory of Sion are the most interesting and long lasting of all the "cults" we have today. Founded in 1099, they are not only the first bankers but are the "fathers" of all the other secret societies or cults such as Freemasonary, the Immunati and Knights Templar. These secret societies still exist today as we will see below in the chapter on World War Two.

To show the knowledge and power these secret societies have, here is a list of three of their members: Leonardo Da Vinci, Isaac Newton and Nostradamus. Galileo (though not known to be a Freemason) was so worried about being killed by the Catholic Church he wrote all his findings in "backwards or mirror writing". The Catholic Church ex-communicated Da Vinci, banned Nostradamus' books and disagreed with Newtons findings regarding gravity and the fact the earth rotated around the sun !!! There were hundreds more Masons (or Freemasons) who were powerful members of society back in the 17th and 18th centuries. Nothing has changed today, especially in the USA, where the Freemasons and other secret societies have ruled for centuries. Lets now look at recent history and the influence of these ancient secret societies that date back to pre Egyptian times. Just before getting into World War Two, lets look at something called "The Protocols". These are a number of ideas or points put forth in the late 1800s' by Freemasons on how they will take over the world. Read them and see if you think they are succeeding.

1) *Wars should not result in territorial gains.*

If you look at the latest wars in Iraq and Afghanastan, you will notice the USA (and allies) did not take over or occupy either country. After nearly a decade in each country, the USA (and allies) simply leave the country and "train" local citizens to run their respective countries. There were territorial gains in World War Two as that was a war between secret societies. (as we will show below)

2) *We shall create a centralization of government. We shall soon begin to create huge monopolies.*

When you consider the media in North America is now almost completely owned by a few families or corporations and the buying and selling of companies has increased substantially in the last decade, its not hard to see where we are headed. Major corporations today control a huge percentage of North American wealth. The same is occuring in Europe.

3) *The increase of police forces in all States of the world so that there is only ourselves and the masses of proletariat, with a few millionaires devoted to our interests, police and soldiers.*

Today we see a lessening of crime year in and year out but yet every year cities hire more and more police. And every year police salaries go up so they are now among the highest paid in society.

Lets take the last G20 meeting in Canada as an example of police powers. On the Saturday, the Black Bloc (known violent anti government protesters) went on a rampage, destroying buildings, police cars and anything else in their way. The police "stood down" as they created havoc yet to this day, nobody will say who gave the order to "stand down". Police admit they had the Black Bloc surrounded but let them go.

The next day (Sunday) police were told to arrest anyone wearing a bandana or "looking suspicious". Thousands were rounded up and jailed for up to 24 hours with no charges brought against them. Some cases are still in court and we still do not have any real answers as to what happened that weekend.

The one thing we did learn was this: The police ran roughshod over a peaceful group of citizens and nothing happened to the police. I encourage people to read the whole newspaper in your city. I can almost guarantee you will see stories every day about police beating, berating, arresting and abusing peoples rights and in virtually 99% of the cases, the police walk free. These stories are usually buried on the back pages.

4) *We have fooled, bemused and corrupted the youth of the masses by rearing them in principels and theories known by us to be false. We shall destroy among the masses the importance of the family and its educational value.*

With 50% of marriages ending in divorce, it looks like this idea has taken root. We also see phonics being replaced in the schools by 'whole reading". This occured after the 1960s generation managed to end the Viet Nam war. The people actually running the world realized young people had become too bright and could now organize themselves and end wars. I will show below how rich families running the world make almost all their money from wars, so it was obvious they had to do something. So, they got rid of phonics, meaning; overall; todays youth do not read as much or as well as past generations.

5) *What is the part played by the press today? We shall saddle and bridle it with a tight curb. Not a single announcement will reach the public without our control.*

See above re a small group now owning and controlling all of the media. As one small example, during the Viet Nam war, we saw nightly newscasts showing the battles. Notice how you never once saw one bit of fighting during the Iraq or Afghanastan wars. Those in power realized the middle class became sickened by the nightly images they saw of war so sided with the hippies over time. Now you will never see any images on newscasts of a current war.

6) *The need for daily bread forces the masses to keep silent and be our humble servants. In order that the masses do not guess what we are really about, we further distract them with games, amusements, sports and other activities.*

After the peace protests of the 1960s, the government began

putting money into building sports stadiums all over America and Europe. Betting became easier to do and sports became a huge draw on television. Suddenly, Sunday sports were allowed. With the advent of video games in the early 80s, governments again put huge money into the building and promoting of these games. When was the last time you saw young girls out skipping rope or a group of young guys playing a pick up game of hockey, football or baseball ? When kids or adults stay inside and play video games, they do not communicate with others and they do not bother with newspapers or reading as much. Just what the government wants. From my experience in the newspaper business, the community newspapers only exist to get flyers into your home.

Also, think about how many jobs are now contract, part time or even interns. In the future, stability will be a thing of the past. Our grandchildren will be at the mercy of the top 1% and we allowed it to happen !

7) *It will be undesirable for us that there should exist any other religion than ours. We must therefore sweep away all other forms of belief.*

Considering the Freemasons and other secret groups consider themselves the direct descendants of the Atlanteans, it is in their interest that we do not believe in Atlantis. So by promoting the Bible, not teaching anything in the school system re Atlantis or Pre-Adamic history, the secret societies keep this ancient knowledge to themselves while teaching "the masses" a watered down version of history. Once they make the final move and take over the world (which is and has been their plan for thousands of years and they know it takes time so are patient) we will then be told they are "a spirit race" and we will in fact be just like the ADAMA. Think back to World War Two. All pictures of Jesus in the schools were replaced by pictures of Hitler. The religion of the Nazis was Nazisim itself. All belief in One God will be forbidden and outlawed. The leader of the government (New

World Order) will be worshipped and treated as "God". For those who think this will not happen, think how close Hitler came to making it possible.

Come to think of it, at the time when the 1% makes their move, I would not be surprised if they allow cloning of humans. We could do it today but countries have outlawed it. Look for that to change.

8) *In our program, one third of the masses will keep the rest under observation from a sense of duty, on the principal of volunteer service to the State. It will be no disgrace to be a spy and informer, but a merit.*

Notice how many cameras are on our streets today? Watching us 24/7. Snitch lines are all the rage these days. Neighborhood watch programs. As noted before, an increase in police officers despite a lessening of crime.

Think about what happens when we have a terrorist attack or threat today. As an example, look at what happened re the Boston Marathon. Although this atrocity was committed by only two brothers, Boston was literally shut down and close to 10,000 heavily armed soldiers are out in the streets. Even then, one brother escaped! Is this possibly used as an excuse to flood the streets with police and the armed forces? Once the public gets used to seeing this kind of activity, it becomes normal. Suddenly, one day the armed forces may not go away !! So much for democracy ! Lets not be so naive as to think this could not happen. If you look at the Protocols, this is *exactly* what will happen.

The Protocols also cover taxation, something that was actually first brought in as a "temporary" measure during World War Two. Here is what they said they would do.

9) *the lawful confiscation of all sums of every kind for the regulation of their circulation in the State. This is to be followed by a progressive tax on property, then a graduated income tax,*

then taxes on sales (sales tax), receipt of moneys, inheritence tax and finally a property transfer tax. Economic crises have been produced by us by withdrawing money from circulation.

Well they certainly followed up well on these ideas. Virtually every form of tax mentioned back in the late 1890s has been instituted (save the tax on inheritence) and I doubt we will have to wait long for that tax to come about. The rich in these secret societies cause recessions by pulling their money from the stock market all at once. Have you ever noticed it takes 5 to 7 years for the stock market to reach a high, then within 3 weeks comes crashing down to maybe 1/3rd of what it was worth just 3 weeks previous? And of course, the rich then re-invest when the market is at its lowest and make a fortune all over again a few years later. The rest of us lose our shirts so have no money to invest when the market is low.

10) *A loan is an issue of government bills of exchange containing an interest charge commensurate to the sum of the loaned capital.*

This simple idea is why the USA currently owes $16 Trillion and virtually every other country in the world is in huge debt. The Mob uses this in their loansharking business. Basically, no matter how much you pay, you always owe the principal. You are only paying off the interest. Here is something even more frightening.

You may have heard the phrase "quantative easing"? Thats a way of saying a country prints money. Right now, most countries are printing money like there is no tomorrow. Of course that means your money becomes worth less because there is more of it out there. To see what happens in this scenario, look at Germany in the late 20s and early 30s. It got to the point where you needed 1 Billion Reichsmarks to buy a loaf of bread. The Reichsmark was replaced by the Deutschmark and Germany suffered way worse during the Depression than other countries. Of course, very few people bother to study history and most people likely figure things like this could never happen today. The secret societies count on this ignorance. It is happening as you read this book !

So there you have the Freemason (Illuminati and other secret societies) blue print for world domination. Personally, I think they are about 80% of the way there.

WORLD WAR TWO:
BATTLE OF THE ATLANTEAN BLOODLINES

Both the Freemasons (the top echelon only) and Illuminati believe they are descended from the Atlanteans. The Nazis also believed the Germans were the direct descendants of the Aryans, one of the Atlantean islands. Both groups frowned on any intermarriage in order to keep the bloodlines pure. As I will show, world war two was simply a battle between these two groups as to who would "carry on" the bloodlines of the Atlanteans. The two groups started working together as the American Freemasons and Illumaniti thought Hitler was the perfect person to run the world (they actually choose Hitler as we will see). Have you ever wondered how Hitler suddenly received so much money in a horrendeous depression? How he obtained food for hundred of thousands Germans virtually overnight? How he obtained the money to buy all the weapons he suddenly produced? Guess no more, he received every penny from the wealthy industrialists in the United States. Prescott Bush, the grandfather of GW Bush, was one of Hitlers main benefactors. Bush loved Hitler from the first time they met in 1924. He went back to the USA and told other influencial people about this man who wanted to destroy unions, destroy communism (which was much more popular in Germany than the Nazis right up until 1928) and was willing to allow the German people to work for peanuts. Considering the intelligence of the Germans (they had developed television by 1929, the theory behind the V1 rocket by 1929 and their films were so advanced, it took Hollywood until the mid 40s before they could re-produce the quality of film the Germans had by the late 1920s) the Americans couldn't wait to utilize their intellegence for low wages so the American industrialists could make even more money.

First, lets take a quick look at the Freemasons / Illuminati and their offshoots to see what they have done over the last 200 years or so.

There are a number of secretive groups in the USA and Britain and Europe who basically run the world. We do not vote for many of them. They are "appointed" to their positions. Bank presidents, leaders of business, ambassadors, leaders of various secret groups such as the Council for Foreign Relations (CFR), Bilderbergers and the Trilateral Commission among many others. Lets look at the Freemasons as an example. By the way, the Freemasons called America "The New Atlantis".

55 of the 56 men who signed the Declaration of Independance were Freemasons. 14 of the 44 Presidents of the USA have been Freemasons. The Freemasons represent less than 1% of the population of any country they have lodges, yet they dominate not only the US political system but most of Europeon Royalty and British leaders. So how is it that a group representing less than 1% of any population can have such immense power? Here is a brief list of some Masons who have lived over the last 250 years:

Winston Churchill, Benjamin Franklin, J Edgar Hoover, Davy Crockett, Mozart, Simon Bolivar, Voltaire, George Washington, Andrew Jackson, Harry Truman, Teddy and Franklin Roosevelt, Paul Revere, John Wilkes Booth (a 33rd degree Mason, the highest position in Freemasonary) and Hubert Humphrey. Quite a list.

Now here is a list of some of the past and present heads of media giants who belonged to secret societies:

William Paley (CBS), John Welsh Jr. (NBC), Thomas Murphy (ABC), Jim Lehrer and Daniel Schorr (PBS), 3 members of Associated Press, Joan Ganz Cooney (Sesame Street and Childrens TV Workshop), W. Thomas Johnson (CNN, Publisher LA Times and member of Freemason LBJs & Rockefeller Foundation Board of Trustees), 4 top executives of both the New

York Times and Time Magazine, 3 top execs at the Washington Post, and two top execs at Readers Digest. So, what are the chances that you are reading what really is happening in the world? This may also explain why you *never* read anything that goes on in the Bilderberg meetings.

Probably one of the most secretive groups is the Federal Reserve of the United States. Believe it or not, the Federal Reserve is not run or owned by the people of the USA nor are any monetary decisions made by the US President. The Federal Reserve is owned by seven families and has been for the last 200 years. (it was named the Federal Reserve in 1913 by the US government but was in existence for at least 100 years previous) They decide how much money can be printed and when it will be printed. And they charge interest on ALL the money they print. So these families make billions from owning the Federal Reserve and put America further and further into debt on a daily basis. Among the families owning the Reserve are the Rothchilds, Morgans, Dunlops, Kolbs and the Roosevelts. It is done through intricate banking systems worldwide. As we will see, these banks loan money to both sides in any war so they profit from all wars and no matter who wins the war, the banking families always win. No matter who is in power, they need money to function and where do they have to go to get the money? You guessed it. Banks! There was a reason Switzerland was never attacked during World War Two. All the money to run the war was deposited there so neither side attacked it.

To show the power of the Federal Reserve, lets look at the only four Presidents who challenged them. President Andrew Jackson announced that the Central Bank in the US was unconstituitional and disbanded it by refusing to charter the bank. There was an attempt on his life soon after by a man named Richard Lawrence. His gun backfired, sparing Jacksons life.

The second was Abraham Lincoln. He was assassinated by John Wilkes Booth, who was a high ranking Freemason as we saw above.

In 1901, President McKinley was assassinated. This was just after he had launched an attack on the Central Bankers and wanted any US money tied to the Gold Standard. The Vice President at the time was Theodore Roosevelt. Once Roosevelt took over, it was easy for the families running the Federal Reserve to get their way once again. Why not, the Roosevelts were one of the biggest benefactors of the Reserve charging interest on any money it created or "loaned" to the USA.

The last President to challenge the Federal Reserve was JFK. He was assassinated by (supposedly) Lee Harvey Oswald. Yet, when District of Attorney Jim Garrison charged Clay Shaw with JFKs murder, Shaws "little black book" showed names such as Stephen Runciman (an expert on Knights Templar and Priory of Sion) who lived in Europe. Shaw also had other prominent Europeons in his address book including royalty such as Princesses (Jacquline Sumay of France), Marquees (Guiseppe Rey of Italy), and Barons, Ladies and Sirs from England. Now why would a man living in New Orleans have these names and numbers in his address book? Supposedly, Shaw was just a businessman. Yet, its obvious he is in tight with Europeon royalty. All of the names were members of the Freemasons or were tied into Europeon banking. Just a coincidence I guess !!! Despite the overwhelming evidence against Clay Shaw, he walked away a free man.

If you read any books on the assassination of JFK, its amazing how many people involved with Oswald are in the CIA, FBI, CFR and other secret outfits. Again, must just be a coincidence !! Think about this: Oswald "defected" to the Soviet Union in 1959 after having been taught how to speak Russian by the American Marines. One reason may be that his accuracy rate in shooting a rifle in marine tests was 51% !! Considering it was claimed Oswald got off three shots in six seconds with a faulty rifle (and hit JFK with 2 of them), you wonder how a man who was a 50 /50 shot at best could suddenly become such an accurate shooter !! Naturally, the marines had no use for a man who was such a lousy shot but he could be used for other purposes.

Once in Russia, Oswald marries a woman named Marina, who lived with her uncle, a high up official in the Russian Internal Ministry. In 1962, at the very height of the Cold War between the US and Russia, Oswald walks back into the States with his Russian wife and is not even stopped for questioning. Just walks back into the USA like he had been to Disneyland for a visit. He then moves into a basement apartment owned by a Mrs. Paine. However, Oswald rents another basement apartment under another name while his wife Marina stays with Mrs. Paine. Mrs. Paine speaks Russian as it turns out. There may have been 200 or so people in all of the USA at that time who could speak Russian so what would the odds be that Oswalds wife moves into a home where the woman speaks Russian? Again, must of just been "luck" that Oswalds Russian speaking wife would rent a place where the woman who owned the property speaks Russian ! Mrs. Paine obtained a job for Lee Oswald as well. It was on the 6th floor of the Book Depository! And lo and behold, witnesses saw a car do a U turn, pick up two "foreign" looking gentlemen and leave the scene of the JFK assassination. A sharp eyed bystander wrote down the plate number. The car belonged to Mrs. Paine ! When questioned she said she lent the car to Lee Oswald for the day. However, not one eyewitness identified Oswald as one of the men in the car. One other odd thing. When reporters tried to obtain Mr. and Mrs. Paines tax filings (they were separated) they were told it was classified information. Why would a supposedly simple woman living in suburban Dallas have her tax reports classified? I would assume the government did not want anyone to know Mrs. Paine worked for either the CIA or the FBI or possibly both.

Here is a quote from J Edgar Hoover two hours after JFK was killed:

"The thing I am concerned about, and so is [Deputy Attorney General Nicholas] Katzenbach, is having something issued so we can convince the public that Oswald is the real assassin." --FBI Director J. Edgar Hoover, speaking on the telephone to Lyndon Johnson aide Walter Jenkins two hours after Oswald was murdered by Jack Ruby, HSCA Report, vol. III, pp. 471-73. (The Warren Commission -- charged with determining the truth in the JFK assassination -- relied upon Hoover's FBI as its primary investigative arm.)

Both Lydon Johnson and J Edgar Hoover were Freemasons. The Warren Commission was made up from various members of the Trilateral Commission (world shadow government), Freemasons and Illuminati. Considering the above statement, is it any wonder how they came to the "conclusion" that Oswald shot JFK.

I recommend a book by Vincent Bugliosi called "Reclaiming History: The Assassination of President John F Kennedy" if you want to study the murder of JFK.

Another sign of the secret societies rule can be seen in the P2 scandal in Italy. Not really covered by the North American media (gee, I don't know why !) this scandal involved the Vatican, the Mob, bankers and some politicians. Ironcially, Silvio Berlusconi was one of the names in secret documents, even though he was not even involved in poltics at the time. Now he has been voted in as Italian PM and even though involved in numerous scandals, still retains high popularity in Italy. Amazing how these well connected people can come from "nowhere" and suddenly are voted into power. As I showed above, the owners and CEOs of all the major media outlets belong or have belonged to the CFR, Freemasons or Trilateral Commission or all three.

I recommend you google P2 scandal to see how in depth this scam was but one of the main people involved was Henry Kissinger. He seems to be involved in many of the backroom decisions made in the USA and Kissinger was a member of the CFR, Trilateral Commission, the Grand Alpine Freemasonary Lodge in Switzerland (which controlled the P2 lodge and masterminded the whole P2 scandal.) He is the only person to attend every Bilderberg Group meeting since 1957.

One more thing to look at: The US one dollar bill. On the back is a pyramid with an eye above it. Both are Masonic images. Why else would they put a pyramid on the one dollar bill? We do not have or build any pyramids in the United States. It also has a Latin phrase on the back of the bill: Novus Ordo Seclorum which in English means "New Worldy Order".

So I think we have seen there are some very powerful people behind the scenes in the United States and elsewhere. And they seem to all be either Freemasons or part of some secretive groups. And one more thing about the Freemasons: They believe they are descended from the Atlanteans and that is why you must have the "correct" bloodlines to ascend up the ladder as a Freemason. Mind you, the vast majority of Freemasons are decent people who have no idea what the top (30th through 33rd level) Freemasons do. To be honest, nobody is supposed to know what they do.

Now that we see how the Freemasons and their ilk control America and Europe, lets look at what the Nazis believed.

The roots of Nazism occur in the later 1800s in Germany. A group called the Thule Society eventually emerged from a hodge podge of radical right wing groups who harboured ideas that included being direct descendants from Atlantis, black magic and sexual deviancy. Founded by a Freemason by the name of Rudolph Von Serbottendorph, this group included members Dietrich Eckart, Alfred Rosenberg, Anton Drexler, Rudolph Hess and other soon to be leading Nazis.

A group called the Skull and Bones; graduates from Yale University; have much in common with the Thule Society. These Skull and Bonesmen have gone on to be Presidents, Vice Presidents and held virtually every major USA high public office (GW Bush had 5 Skull and Bonesmen as his top aides) . Here is one example of how the Skull and Bones operate:

"...*Members of the Order (Skull and Bones) take an oath that absolves them from any allegiance to any nation or king or government or constitution, and that includes the negating of any subsequent oath which they may be required to take. They swear allegiance only to the Order and its goal of a New World Order...according to the oath Bush (speaking of the first president Bush) took when he was initiated into Skull and Bones, his oath of office as President of the United States means nothing."*

Note that both Bush Presidents talked about a "New World Order". Hitler continually spoke about the Nazis being a "New World Order" that would rule for 1,000 years. Note also the Bible talks about Jesus coming back to earth and starting a 1,000 year cycle of peace. Is this once again the Sons of Belial (Nazis, Skull and Bones) against the Law of One (those who believe in God)? Time will tell. I know GW Bush claimed to be a Christian but not any Christians I know would start two major wars, be a "heavy drinker" (Bushs own words) and a cocaine abuser until age 40. To his credit, GW Bush did clean up his personal life.

After World War One, Germany was in a shambles. Communism was becoming popular and the industrialists in Germany were frightened the Communists would take over and nationilize their businesses. They got together and decided to bring together the eight most popular right wing parties in Germany at that time. They needed a leader for this new party and decided on a bachelor "war hero" named Adolph Hitler. I put war hero in brackets as Hitler was actually a draft dodger who was captured and sent to the front in world war one. The Germans did this as virtually nobody on the front lines survived the war. Every single man in Hitlers battalion was killed except for Adolph Hitler. Although severely injured, Hitler recovered from his injuries and was given work as a spy. His job was to infiltrate start up German political parties. One party was the (soon to be) Nazis. Consisting of six homosexual men, the party was just a front to hide their sexual orientation. However, Hitlers bosses told him to return to the next meeting where Hitler was offered the post of leader. Laughing it off, Hitler was surprised when his handlers told him to take the job. From there, the industrialists merged the other parties behind this small group and poured money into the party. As an aside, Hitler had most of the homosexual members of the Nazi Party murdered during the Night of 1,000 Knives in June of 1934.

As it turned out, Hitler had read all the street posters pasted around Austria during his five years living as a street bum. That's right, Hitler spent five long years living in mens shelters, wandering the streets by day, starving and ranting about what he would do when he became leader. When he became leader, he met with his old homeless friend and reminded the man (his name was August Kubizek) about his ideas. The members of the press say Mr. Kubizek looked extremely ill while reminsicing with Hitler. Considering Hitler had told August during his rantings that he would kill all the Jews, take control of the whole world and make the workers no better than slaves, it is no wonder Mr. Kubizek felt a little ill.

Anyways, Hitler had realized the value of these street posters and flyers and decided this was the way to win power. Remember, this is the early 1920s before TV or radio in Germany, so flyers delivered door to door and posted on polls was very effective advertising. For that matter, flyers are still the mainstay of community newspapers to this day.

As mentioned above, most insider Nazis were all members of the

Thule Society and Hitler eagerly accepted their views regarding Jews (whom Hitler already disliked), the Germans being the Aryan race and sexual deviancy. The four women Hitler had relations with all committed suicide. These women were Inga Ley (committed suicide Dec, 1942), Renata Muller (committed suicide October of 1937), Eva Braun (committed suicide with Hitler in 1945) and Geli Raubal, Hitlers niece, who jumped to her death in September of 1931. There are various rumours as to Hitlers deviances but I will not get into that here. Again, I encourage people to google any information they would like to follow up on.

The only reason Hitler became Chancellor was due to 39 business leaders signing a petition asking Von Hindenburg to put Hitler in charge. There had been 5 elections between 1928 and 1933 and the business leaders claimed the country could not afford another election, so why not appoint Hitler, who came second. Hitler never won an election in Germany. Hitler assumed power in 1933, had the Reichstag burnt down almost immediately, blamed it on the Communists and went on a murderous rampage, killing any and all Communist members he could capture.

Hitler also had the help of an American businessman named Prescott Bush. His son and grandson would go on to become US Presidents. In the 1920s, Bush was in Germany and after meeting Hitler, returned to the US praising Hitler and encouraging industrialists to help fund Hitlers new party.

During the building up of the Nazi Party, Hitler had contact and received money from the worlds top industrialists. All of the fuel for the Nazi Luftwaffe was supplied by America, including all fuel used during World War Two. This was done through third parties and moving the money through banks to hide where the fuel (and money) were coming from. Read the book "Rule by Secrecy" by Jim Marrs to find out much more about this and other secret societies over the centuries.

Here is another interesting story regarding Hitlers background. His grandmother (last name Schicklgruber) was a maid in the home of one of the Rothchilds. She had an illegitimate child that was thought to be fathered by Mr. Rothchild. This child was named Alios and he was Adolph Hitlers father !! It also might account for why he was choosen to be the leader of the Nazi Party and why all the money was put behind him. Of course, this also means Hitler had 25% Jewish blood.

Hitlers father was 51 when his wife (his 2nd cousin) became pregnant. Between his old age and inter marriage, was this possibly why his son Adolph Hitler went basically insane?

Henry Ford supplied trucks to Germany well into the second world war. He was known to dislike Jewish people and never hired any Jews in his plants. Ford actually believed in the "Jewish conspiracy" to control the world so did everything in his power (including buying a newspaper, the Dearborn Independant) to promote his "theories". Ironically, the Germans never really caught onto Fords products and his sales in Germany were weak compared to other areas of the world.

Now you are probably asking, why did the Freemasons in America turn against Hitler? The answer is simple. When Rudolph Hess flew to Scotland to propose a peace treaty, Hitler felt he was a traitor and began to wonder if Hess (a long time member of the Thules and believer in the Germans being Atlanteans) was part of some secret society that he (Hitler) was not aware of. Hitler immediately issued a decree: All secret society members in Germany; and elsewhere; would be locked up or killed as soon as possible.

The Freemasons realized Hitler was not only insane but was already rounding up and killing millions of Jews, so how hard would it be for Hitler to round up the Freemasons and kill them as well? World War Two was on !

The first big problem for the USA was they had used their ownership of the press to convince Americans that the war was simply a 'Europeon War" and the US should stay out of it. It worked so well that over 80% of Americans were against entering the war. Now what could they do to change the minds of American citizens? It didnt take long to come up with a solution.

Intelligence reports showed Japan was getting ready to attack the USA. The Japanese were running low on oil and other necessary items to run a war and realized the only way to get them was through the USA. Once they had decided to get rid of Hitler, the US industrialists cut off all supplies to Japan and Germany. Well, all except one: Prescott Bush. (grandfather to GW and father of George Bush Sr.) He owned a company called the Union Banking Corporation. The other owners were E. Roland Harriman and 4 Nazi Party members. These four were Albert Voegler, Fritz Thyssen, Hjalmar Schacht and Friedrich Flick. The US govermment took over the bank and all four Germans were eventually charged. Prescott Bush and Harriman walked away. It is interesting to note that while his son and grandson spent 12 years running the US government, not once did any media outlet ever talk about Prescotts past. Also note, both Bush Presidents talked incessantly about a "New World Order". It should be noted as well that Prescott Bush got his start through the Harriman family and both were involved in the eugenics (cleansing bloodlines) studies in the early to mid 20th century. The first international Congress of Eugenics was held in London in 1912 and the Vice President of the Congress was none other than Winston Churchill !!

This shows how the Freemasons and secret societies believed the same thing the Nazis did: They were descended from the Atlanteans and wanted to "cleanse" the blood make a "pure race".

With this news regarding a potential attack on Pearl Harbour, the top officials in the US White House decided not to say anything and allow the attack to take place. They discreetly moved as many airplanes out of the area as they could, as they knew this war would be won in the air, not at sea or on land. Naturally, after the attack, American citizens were outraged and ready for war against Japan and Germany.

At the end of the war, the Nuremburg Trials took place. Notice they never once brought up the Nazis belief in Atlantis, bloodlines or occult practices or any of the basic beliefs of the Nazis. I wonder why ! It seems odd since Winston Churchill himself was the Vice President of the Congress looking into eugenics in 1912 in England.

Moving forward from World War Two, suddenly the Communists are no longer our allies but our enemy. The Korean War, the Viet Namese war are all ideological wars. Then when Communism disappears overnight (as Edgar Cayce had predicted by the way), suddenly Islam and Muslims are our enemy. Why is it the USA always has to have an enemy? It wouldn't be so the secret societies and Federal Reserve can make billions of dollars would it?

If you look at 9/11, 15 of the 19 hijackers are from Saudi Arabia. Yet the USA attacks Iraq. Why? The UN had attacked and taken all of the weapons away from Saddam Hussein in the early 90s, yet now GW Bush claims they have "weapons of mass destruction" and orders an invasion. Of course, two years later, whoops, there are no weapons of mass destruction but since we are already at war............

Then the USA attacks Afghanistan because they "thought' Osama Bin Laden lived there. Turns out he lived in Pakistan when the Obama administration catches and kills him. For the last seven years of the Bush administration they could not seem to find Osama Bin Laden ! Of course, when you fly 9 members of the Bin Laden family out of the USA the day after their brother has orchestrated the murder of 3.000 Americans, you wonder exactly what is going on. Why would the Bush administration not hold the family members until at least interviewing them about where their brother might be?

Also, George Bush Sr. and Osama Bin Ladens brother were in a hotel room a few blocks from the Pentagon watching the planes hit. They were attending a meeting of the Carlyle Group, a company that has basically bought up the defense companies world wide. Haliburton is tied into the Carlyle Group and guess who received most of the contracts to rebuild Iraq and Afghanastan? If you guessed Haliburton, congrats. And who was one of the top guns in Haliburton? Dick Cheney, the man who orchestrated both wars. What a coincidence.

Ironically, when Ronald Reagan had the attempt on his life, John Hinckleys brother (Hinckley was the man who tried to shoot Reagan) had dinner that night with Neil Bush, George Srs. son. Makes you wonder if somehow these secret societies have some kind of code where when they pull some major event, they have two family members involved get together to show solidarity? It definitely makes you wonder. Also, the Vice President during Reagans reign was George Bush Sr. !! I guess they couldn't wait until George could be elected ! However, after this, Reagan stayed in power his full 8 years. Ironically, George Bush Sr. only lasted one term. Bill Clinton won the next election but since Clinton was tied to the Freemasons, not too much changed behind the scenes. Clinton also belonged to the CFR, the Trilateral Commission and the Bilderbergs.

As you can see, for some reason the USA attacks and starts wars for little or no reason. I wonder why? Well, just as always, the bankers and secret socities make billions upon billions from wars so they make sure the USA has "enemies" and make sure a war gets started. Notice how the USA just never seems to be able to end these wars quickly. The Viet Nam was waged for 10 years. The Iraq war dragged on for 10 years and the Afghan war is now more than 10 years old. You wonder how a powerful country like the USA could not end the wars relatively quickly. Unless, of course, there are people who do not want the war to end quickly !

Who could those people be? I will leave it up to the reader to decide if they think there may be a reason the USA enters so many wars. I honestly do not think the citizens of the USA want these wars.

Another interesting thing with the Freemasons are the numbers 11, 22 and 33. Although once again a fairly far out theory, let me just present a few things that have the number 33. As I mentioned near the beginning of the book, virtually all of the ancient buildings were at or near the 33rd parallel. There are 33 strands of DNA in the human body. Returning spacecraft sent up by the USA land on runway 33. This would seem inconsequential except for the number of astronauts who were Masons and Freemasons. Here is a list: Buzz Aldrin (who took a Mason flag to the moon and brought it back to be hung at the Temple in Texas where he belonged to the Masons), Gordon Cooper (who took a Scottish Mason flag on his trip in 1965), Gus Grissom, Walter Schirra and Edgar Mitchell. Many of the leaders of NASA were Freemasons so this is likely why the runway was numbered 33. There are only a few runways so you have to wonder why they would pick a high number like 33 as the runway number.

There are 33 vertabrae in a humans body. Jesus died at age 33. The first world war ended on the 11th month, on the 11th hour of the 11th day. That adds up to 33. JFK was killed on the 11 month on the 22nd day. (adds up to 33). The Masons had a lodge in the Dealey Plaza by the way. Robert Kennedy was murdered at the Ambassador Hotel, located near the 33rd parallel and right beside a Masonic Temple. The Bible is full of references to the number 33. The Bible claims the highest level a Man can reach is the 33rd level of Spirituality. In the Mystery schools, initiates had to go through 3 levels, 3 times. Even Roswell, New Mexico is on the 33rd parallel. That was where a space ship supposedly crashed. FDR died at Warm Springs Georgia which is at the 33rd parallel. (his medical report went missing). He was replaced by Harry Truman, who was a 33rd level Mason. Truman then dropped a bomb on Nagasaki, which is at the 33rd parallel.

Just another interesting fact and again, I encourage readers to google this kind of information to see what you can find.

In conclusion, lets look at a statement from Ecclesiastes 1:9 to 1:11 in the Bible. Here it is:

History merely repeats itself. It has all been done before. Nothing under the sun is truly new. What can you point to that is new? How do you know it did not exist long ago? We do not remember what happened in those former times. And in future generations, no one will remember what we are doing now".

Despite all its hidden meaning, in this case the Bible is clear, concise and accurate.

I think the story I have told here proves there was a Pre-Adamic era not covered; or at least hidden; by the writers of the Bible. As we discover more artifacts from around the world, and we see more incredible inventions every day, we begin to realize what we were taught in schools was not correct. Adam and Eve were not the first people nor did God create them. Columbus did not "discover" America. There is a small, powerful,wealthy group of people intent on taking over mankind. They almost succeeded during World War Two. They are still working today towards their goal of complete domination of the world.

I suppose the reality is this: Can we overcome greed, jealousy, hate and selfishness and become once again a Spirit Race? Or will we continue on the path of destruction and have to start over from the beginning?

If we are destroyed as a civilization and basically start over, how many generations will it take before space travel, television, atomic bombs, cloning and all the other modern conveniences we have are considered myths?

There seems little doubt we are on the cusp of incredible discoveries in medicine, space exploration and past history. Unfortunately, we are also on the cusp of destroying ourselves or allowing ourselves to be overtaken by a small group of people intent on ruling us with an iron fist and turning us into modern day ADAMA.

Only time will tell and time seems to be running out. Thank you for reading and again, please google any and all the information you see here and make up your own mind on both our past and future.